ACCOUNTABLE

ACCOUNTABLE

An Inspirational Approach to Re-Engage Your People and Achieve Greater Success

Peter Myers, P.Eng., MA

MESH Mesh Organizational Services

The names and identifying characteristics of some of the individuals featured throughout this book have been changed to protect their privacy.

Additional books can be purchased for educational, business or sales promotional use. For information please email;

accountable@mesh.team.

Mesh website: http://mesh.team

ISBN 978-0-9952677-0-1

First Edition

10 9 8 7 6 5 4 3 2 1

Acknowledgements

The writing of a book and the starting of a consulting business is a long difficult challenge that is doomed to failure without the support of many, many people. The starting of Mesh Organizational Services and the writing of ***Accountable*** has been more challenging than I could have ever imagined.

I want to thank everyone who has ever helped me to understand the importance of people and inspired me to work hard, empower others and never get too complacent. Specifically, I want to thank the following people;

Alicia Milner – Your support and attention to detail has helped me immensely over the last few years. I have always appreciated your care, concern, and ideas throughout this journey.
Alison Thom – I know that the last few years have been very difficult, and it has been tough to rely on me at times, but I really appreciate everything you have done to compensate for my absence. You are one hell of a great mom.
Bill Baillie – Your friendship and your approach to solving challenges and living life have always been a great inspiration for me. Thanks for your invaluable input and feedback.
Boris Clark and Karen Miendinger – Thank you so much for taking care of me while in the Yukon and letting me stay at the "writer's retreat" to work on the book!
Dave and Jude Liderth – Whether providing me with feedback at Disaster Inc. board meetings, challenging me on my theories or offering me a place to sleep when I needed it, it's great to have good friends.
Dave Boone (#43) – Thanks for sharing your experience, your compassion and the odd slash across the shins! You really helped me to figure out what I was doing and what my value proposition is.
Dorothy Miller – I greatly appreciated the time we spent together Masterminding, keeping me moving in the right direction and always staying positive.
Doug and Doran Myers – Family relationships are always the ones that suffer most during any business startup. You are the two most amazing children a man could ask for. I love you and thank you for the sacrifices you've made for me!

Fraser Godfrey – Thanks for giving me your perspectives on my book and my approach. Getting real-world feedback has helped me make the book much more relevant and engaging.
Gerry LeBlanc – Thanks for inspiring me to stay the course and not be afraid to take on the elephant in the boardroom.
Ivan Hui – Thanks for your insights and perspectives on making the book a more powerful force for positive change.
James Malinchak – Thanks for inspiring me to do more, to reach higher and to always approach challenges with a positive mindset.
Jay Cummings – When you take the journey of an entrepreneur, often old friends don't understand because you're taking a different path than they did. Thanks for knowing me and believing in me. I love you!
Jeff Myers – You have always been there for me, even as a kid. Thanks bro!
Jess & Lina Huffman and all the amazing people at The Bridge – Finding The Bridge CoWorking space was a godsend. Thanks for everything you have done for me, the book and my business.
Jill Smolkin – Inspiration comes in many forms and your positive energy and enthusiastic feedback are exactly what this beleaguered entrepreneur needed to give me the energy not to just cross the finish line but charge across it full of expectancy and confidence.
John Addy – If it wasn't for Disaster Inc, this book likely would have never been written. Thanks for your insights, perspectives, and support.
John Branigan – it was great to reconnect. I have and will continue to always appreciate your frank feedback.
Marc Robertson & Janel Wageman – When someone starts their business, their goal is not to lose everything and then rely on your friends for support but that is what happened, and this business could not have gotten off the ground without your generosity…Thanks.
Neville Chamberlain – thanks for your help getting clarity on my business model…it takes a long time and a lot of patience! You're a great coach…all the best with Britewrx (https://britewrx.com).
Rob Pearce – Your input really helped me to turn the corner in the creation of my accountability framework. Thanks for your interest and support.
Susan Cramer – Thanks for your ability to organize, coordinate and keep it real. You are a great sounding board with a wealth of knowledge and experience. Best of luck with S2 Seminars. (http://s2seminars.ca/)

Trevor and Lisa Thompson – Having someone to talk to; to listen and to offer me advice has helped me more than anything else get through the last three years. Thanks for always being there for me!
Tuesday Nooner Toastmasters – What an incredible, insightful and supportive group of mentors who have helped me to have confidence in my voice and in my message.

Lastly, I want to acknowledge all the friends and acquaintances, that I have shared conversations with about accountability, helping me to shape my words, my language, and my vision.

Dedication

Accountable is dedicated to all the people that listened to me, supported me and believed in me. I'm still trying to make a difference and I hope you are too!

Contents

1. Introduction........ 10
2. Bully in the Workplace........ 14
3. The Accountability Crisis........ 21
4. The Root of the Problem: Accountability........ 28
5. Accountability: The Leading Indicator of Success...... 33
6. Why Change Now?........ 38
7. The Quest for Accountability........ 50
8. Barriers to Accountability........ 62
   a) Too Much Chaos........ 63
   b) Lack of Inspirational Leadership........ 67
   c) Lack of understanding........ 69
   d) Lack of Initiative........ 72
   e) Lack of Authority........ 74
   f) Lack of Process........ 77
   g) Too Much Process........ 78
   h) Lack of Competency........ 81
   i) Lack of Time........ 84
   j) Lack of Transparency........ 86
   k) Lack of Confidence........ 88
   l) Heroism........ 90
   m) Micromanagement........ 92
9. Guiding Values of Accountability........ 95
10. Changing to an Accountable Culture........ 104

Notes........ 114

About the Author........ 118

1. Introduction

> *"There's been a quantum leap technologically in our age, but unless there's another quantum leap in human relations, unless we learn to live in a new way towards one another, there will be a catastrophe."*
>
> *Albert Einstein*
>
> *German physicist, scientific philosopher and Nobel prize winner*

In the summer of 1998, I was a Tooling Engineer working at Chrysler Canada's Pillette Road Truck Assembly Plant. We used to make just under 100,000 full-size Dodge Ram vans each year (one every 60 seconds while the plant was operating) and it was rumored that the corporation made close to $10,000 per vehicle, the most profitable per vehicle rate in their fleet.

But sales were slumping, and the vehicle needed an overhaul. Major retooling programs are massively expensive, so the head honchos in Detroit decided a modest facelift to improve its curb appeal and user interfaces would give the van the edge it needed to increase sales.

I worked in the trim department and was responsible for all tooling required to assemble all vehicle interior components, lights, windows and body moldings. The re-tooling program would include significant changes to the instrument panel (IP) and dashboard including a completely new IP subassembly line, interior upgrades, and a new steering wheel, however, the body would stay the same.

The plant had an old school, top-down management style where decision-making authority had migrated up to a few key individuals at the top of the local leadership team. There was a strong resistance to change and a common rebuttal to any new ideas and suggestions was, "We don't need to change anything! That's the way we've been doing it for 20 years and it's been working fine!"

I really enjoyed my job, working with the skilled trades to solve problems, improve the quality of the vehicle and deal with ergonomic or efficiency issues to support the workers on the line. But I hated the lack of respect I received from my managers. I was a unionized engineer and was shocked by how differently I was treated because I was in the union. I even volunteered to move to the afternoon shift, so I would only have to put up with the games and abuse for a couple hours at the beginning of my shift then I could get to work. At Chrysler, it seemed that respect only flowed one way…up!

The retooling, as it's called, was not a massive project, but nonetheless, the changes entailed significant spending…the budget for my work alone was over $1,000,000. I was one Tooling Engineer in one department of one area, so during the eight-week shutdown, tens of millions of dollars would be spent, and hundreds of small projects would have to be completed, requiring a highly integrated and organized high-performance project team, committed to the tasks, timing, and allocation of limited resources across the entire plant.

For our first project meeting, there were 60 people in attendance. The corporate guys, the operations folks, the product people, the engineers and the labor representatives all assembled around a massive square of folding tables in a temporary office that had been built in the back of the plant. The Corporate Project Manager (CPM) began to outline the agenda for the meeting but was quickly interrupted by the Plant Project Manager (PPM).

"Excuse me, but this is my meeting…it's my responsibility to set the agenda and lead this meeting," he insisted.

"Well I am responsible for this project," the CPM retorted. "And I need this meeting to address some key concerns I have with the progress of the project."

He began to list his key agenda points and again was interrupted by the PPM. "I will be damned if I'm going to let you come into my plant and try to take over!"

"This a corporate project and I am in charge and will tell you what the agenda is, and you will god damn well listen!!" the CPM shouted.

They went on for over half an hour, yelling and cursing at each other.

The rest of us looked on in a state of utter disbelief. I was a lowly Tooling Engineer and although tempted to speak up several times, knew it would not be appropriate. I scanned the table to see who might be willing to say something to get this meeting back on track. There were a couple of corporate managers who could have stepped in but didn't. The Operations Manager, the senior representative from the plant sat motionless, clearly having decided that stepping in might not have been the best move on his part.

Finally, the plant Safety Lead, one of the key members of the plant's unionized workforce stood up and said, "When you decide who's meeting it is, let me know," and he walked out.

And so went the project…continuous conflict, mean-spirited micromanagement, bullying and intimidation, crazy levels of stress and a constant fight for power, control, and access to resources. We had no uniting vision of success or sense of collaboration. We knew what our deadline was and there was never any question that we would make it, despite ourselves and the chaos swirling around us.

We went back into production on schedule and the project was likely hailed as a great success. But it wasn't. It was a disaster! We had no sense of victory or achievement, and we had paid a heavy price with bruised egos, hard feelings and stress levels ratcheted up to maximum. It felt like we had aged several years during those hectic few weeks.

Since my experience on that project, I knew that there had to be a better way. A way that understood the importance of a unified and committed team that eliminated micromanagement and bullying and replaced it with organization, leadership, respect, and accountability.

Accountable is a practical guide to help organizations realize more value from their people but more importantly, is a rallying cry to fundamentally rethink our traditional top-down management style and create work environments that have clarity of purpose, integration of systems, alignment of resources and empowerment of people.

I believe in the power of people and I think too many organizations, whether multinational corporations, government bodies, locally owned business or not-for-profits try to control people rather than setting them up to be the best they can be…highly competent, innovative, customer-driven value centers.

The book looks at workplace trends that are challenging the traditional top-down management model, pushing it to a tipping point where the risk reduction practice of keeping decision-making authority in the hands of a few has stripped the organization of its agility to react to market forces and compete on a global scale.

As you enter discussions on accountability, you will find many perspectives, assumptions, and beliefs on what it is and how it works, many of which do not support a powerful perspective of accountability. ***Accountable*** creates a more powerful and unifying vision of what accountability is and what holds us back as individuals and organizations from realizing the tremendous benefits of an accountable workforce.

I define accountability as;

> "Meeting or exceeding customer and stakeholder needs and expectations."

This quality-centric definition ensures everything we do is focused on producing high-quality consistent interactions and outputs, which act as repeatable inputs to our customers' and stakeholders' processes.

With a focus on accountability, your organization can achieve much greater levels of success and your employees and volunteers can achieve a much greater sense of personal achievement.

People generally don't want to retire and look back at their career and say, "I could have done better; I could have done more; I could have made a difference, but it was just easier to do what I was told."

Accountable is for those of you who know there is a better way and who are striving to transform their organizations into high-performance customer service centers and provides the tools and perspectives you will need to better understand what accountability is and how it can be used as a leading indicator of organizational success.

2. Bully in the Workplace

> "I allowed myself to be bullied because I was scared and didn't know how to defend myself. I was bullied until I prevented a new student from being bullied. By standing up for him, I learned to stand up for myself."
>
> Jackie Chan
> Martial artist, actor, director, producer, stuntman

Ever since I was in grade school, I had a reputation for standing up to bullies; those mean-spirited individuals that push people around and try to always get their way through coercion, intimidation or violence. I never backed down to bullies. In fact, when someone would begin to act like a bully, I was usually right there to challenge them, to call them out and to be ready to dodge the punch when it came.

I was not a fighter although not afraid of a fight, so I typically pushed back with my words, sometimes using logic, sometimes using persuasion and sometimes, bullying right back and showing them that I was not going to back down. And if the fist came, I was pretty good at throwing them into one of my big-time wrestling submission holds until they calmed down!

In school, often the biggest bullies were the teachers and again, I became adept at using my words to stand up to them and call them out on their bad behavior. One such individual was my high school math teacher. After having several confrontations and conflicts throughout the school year, including a fight in a student/teacher hockey game, he falsified my final exam mark, lowering my math mark to a point that would have prevented me from being accepted into engineering school.

Trying to use your position of authority to alter the trajectory of someone's life (in a negative way) is low but that is what bullies do when you stand up to them. They quickly drop all facades of values and ethics and focus on how they can get revenge.

I called him out on it and made him pull my final exam (we weren't given a copy of the final exam, so he could reuse the same test year after year after year). Buried in a 3-foot stack of exams in his locker, we eventually found it and surprise, surprise, my mark was 85%, not the 55% he had recorded on my final report. If I had been too afraid or intimidated by him to not call him out and demand to see my final exam mark, my life would have been very different.

Of course, if I had never stood up him, he would not have sought revenge against me. Standing up to bullies is not easy or without its cost, but if we don't stand up to them, they take over and do what's good for them with little regard for others. They degrade the values and ethics of our organizations and our society and they enable others to become bullies, further degrading our ability to create win-win solutions to our challenges.

When I graduated and began my career in engineering and project management, I found the workplace was filled with bullies who had landed in a new home after graduating from high school, college or university. But unlike the schoolyard bullies, who really had no power over you, workplace bullies had position, power, and authority over others and used that position of authority to unduly influence decisions to meet their needs regardless of the negative impacts to individual stakeholders or even the company, as long as they benefitted.

My ability to push back was severely limited. It seems in the workplace, truth, circumstance and due diligence are meaningless concepts if the bullies are in a position of authority or are well connected to the organizational leadership. No amount of negotiation, persuasion or logic could sway them from their course of retribution. They didn't let simple things like facts get in the way of the punishment that they would eventually deliver.

That inability to stand up to workplace bullies severely affected me in the early years of my career. I would get increasingly frustrated with directives and orders that did not take the needs of others into consideration. I have always been strong in relationship building so if I let the people down whom I was supposed to be serving, I couldn't live with myself.

Other times, my managers imposed unworkable solutions and then criticized and blamed me when what they told me to do was wrong. Or worse yet, reprimanded me for doing something different than they told me even though what I did worked and was the right thing to do.

I knew I could not survive in a workplace where bullying was the norm and at several points in my career considered simply walking away from it all. I certainly walked away from many of them (and was fired from several others) but always ended up somewhere else that seemed an awful lot like the place I had left.

When I started to manage my own projects, I figured that was my chance to get ahead of the bullies and not let them try to take over. To do that, I met with key stakeholders and ensured that their needs were documented. I ran responsibility workshops, so we had clarity on who would be doing what and what the limits of those responsibilities were. I marked up drawings to indicate what real estate was being allocated to various stakeholders during certain times of the construction project. I used the company's values statement to reinforce appropriate behavior and asked for support from the powers that be when people didn't live up to those values.

I definitely had some success with my approach in the early days but still recognized that mean-spirited micromanagers and workplace bullies often didn't follow the rules or espoused values and were never reprimanded for it. My management team simply did not have the authority (or the backbone) to deal with it and impose consequences when people didn't live up to the team's expectations.

On a subsequent project, I was able to isolate my team from the rest of the organization and again my goal was to create an inspiring work environment that gave them the clarity of purpose, task, and process they needed to take ownership of their responsibilities. But this time, I included a high-performance team process that ensured that people were committed to the vision of the organization, to the goals of the project, to the needs and expectations of the client, and to each other; understanding that we would succeed together or fail together.

I was not able to turn mean-spirited people into collaborative do-gooders, but I was able to get most of my team to not only buy-into the approach but embrace it as their own. That left a couple outliers who thought my approach was "a waste of time". I have since found that the "waste of time" refrain is a consistent theme with bullies and micromanagers who thrive in a more chaotic, less planned work environment. It turns out, a strong team culture is the greatest deterrent to workplace bullying and poor performance!

By creating clarity on who was responsible for what I was able to set boundaries for responsibilities and get agreement on who their customers and stakeholders were, including identifying their needs and expectations.

One of the outliers was my electrical lead who was notorious for doing things how he wanted them and displaying an arrogance that challenged anyone who questioned his approach, even if that approach was clearly in violation of the customer's or team members expectations.

During the early stages of the project, he had provided the material list on which part of our project cost estimate was based, and my expectation was that he would stand behind the material list by signing off on the final estimate. (btw: this person had a reputation for making up initial material lists and then making massive changes to it when the design was finalized, resulting in significant cost increases on most of his projects).

He refused, claiming that he could not be responsible for the pricing in the estimate. I completely agreed and acknowledged that my expectation was that his sign off meant that he agreed only with the materials quantities within the estimate, not the final cost of those items. But he still refused and then walked off my project declaring that he could not work for a tyrant like me (bullies often accuse others of being bullies when people stand up to them).

And although his departure created many challenges, it also created opportunities to improve the relationship with the client. They were frustrated with his tendency to ignore their requests and were delighted that he had walked and so was I. It was much easier to maintain a cohesive team without people who refused to be accountable to the client and our team.

But the departure of my electrical lead raised a flag to our company's executive team. They questioned why a 35-year guy, who they had never had a problem with, walked off my team? There had to be something wrong with Pete! They began questioning people on my team looking for faults and reasons to terminate me. But my team stood behind me and suggested I was doing a great job.

They then went to the client, suggesting I be terminated as my project was clearly failing, the proof of which was the departure of the electrical lead. The client listened to their concerns then made a clear statement to our company ownership, "Terminate Pete and we terminate the contract!" end of conversation. One of my greatest learnings in project management is to make sure your team and your client trusts you and know that you are looking out for their best interests. It's often the only protection you have from the bullies within your own organization.

Because I was able to stand up for our team and the bigger vision that we held, I gained tremendous credibility, and the reward for that was an increasing willingness to live up to the team processes that I had integrated. They began to challenge each other when their own needs and expectations were not being met or when a teammate wasn't living up to their commitments. People were delivering more, and they were demanding more. But they did it in a collaborative way, using positive language to raise their concerns and verbalize how the breakdown would impact them in terms of their own commitments. We always stayed positive and supportive with a clear focus on the goals of the project and the team.

And because I was able to chase the bullies off my team, I was able to get people to be more committed to success and accountable to others. I was able to fix the broken document management system which then resulted in field rework being reduced by 95%. I was able to build trust with my teammates and create a powerful collaborative team that our client also trusted. They then gave us the space we needed to be innovative in our design resulting in a final product that not only met the service requirements of the project but developed a great sense of buy-in and commitment by the people in Operations and Maintenance because their needs and expectations had been factored into the design.

Far too many organizations use the "one throat to choke" approach to accountability, meaning that one person is responsible for the work of many. As a result, the many take no responsibility or ownership, they are simply doing what they have been told. Micromanagers dictate decisions, feeling they are the ones who will be punished if things go wrong. Sadly, being removed from the work face, they often don't understand the complexity of the situation or the needs of the customer or stakeholders and end up with self-serving solutions that create chaos and reduce value for other stakeholders.

Accountability is a much more powerful tool, if we move upstream. Stop focusing on the one throat to choke when things go wrong and instead focus on the quality, consistency, and precision of interactions within your team as an early indicator of potential breakdowns with your customers. If the front-line employee is handed something that does not meet their needs and will not meet the needs of the customer, they must either a) ask the other employee to rework the item; b) rework the previous employees work themselves, or c) pass on the mistake.

An accountable culture would push the rework back to the originator and would ask for ways to prevent the deviation from occurring again. The owner of the work must then be empowered by their management team to solve the problem and implement the solution that would prevent them from suffering from poor quality again.

Many organization's accountability breaks down when they fail to provide the resources necessary to fix the problems, leaving the person doing the task feeling no accountability to their stakeholders for the inferior quality of the work.

Moving to a culture of accountability is the single biggest decision an organization can make to go from good to great. And it's likely the easiest organizational change you will take on because the vast majority of your people will support the transformation, with the possible exception of some of the heroes, bullies, and micro-managers. By providing clarity to my team on my needs and expectations, and implementing quality assurance processes to monitor them, I was able to able to nip bully behavior in the bud, before it could have lasting negative impacts on the success of my project.

Most importantly, accountability must start at the top. If upper management is fuzzy on their responsibilities, that fuzziness grows as you descend the organizational chart, resulting in increasing levels of chaos, frustration, and incivility. If you simply try imposing accountability on your staff without being accountable yourself, accountability, and results, will not improve.

Many organizations are using bolt-on policies to address human resource issues, but they often have little effect if they do not address the underlying issues of workplace bullying; poor accountability. Organizations can beat workplace bullying, but they must be willing to adopt an accountable culture.

The following chapters will give you the tools you will need to begin your organizational transformation.

3. The Accountability Crisis

> *"But accountability has never been more important because, for far too many of us, our very livelihoods are at stake."*
>
> \- Sarah Kate Ellis
> GLADD CEO
> on the Trump Accountability Project

I recently listened to Donald Trump speak at a pre-meeting to his big United Nations (UN) Assembly speech. He spoke quite openly and eloquently about the need to reform the UN. He pointed out, without being too abrasive, that it had become a dysfunctional, bureaucratic establishment with little impact, willingness or ability to carry out its mandate. He accused its leadership and management of lacking accountability. Smartest thing the man ever said!

The problem is, the UN can't fix itself, just like Donald Trump is learning he can't fix the dysfunctional, bureaucratic establishments within his own country. Or at least, not with his top-down command and control management style that relies heavily on intimidation, bullying, manipulation and fake news. Accountability starts at the top and if the President of the United States wants other organizations to be more accountable to him as a stakeholder, then he has to start being more accountable to them. That means being inclusive, not divisive; being collaborative, not competitive; being inspiring, not demanding.

The Boys Club, Command and Control, Top-down…whatever you call it…is an almost monopolistic management style employed worldwide, across capitalist establishments, government departments, volunteer organizations and religious orders.

In an ongoing study conducted by LRN and the Boston Research Group, (The HOW Report[1]), it found that only 8% of companies were identified as "Self-Governing". These are organizations whose governance embraces social responsibility and long-term goals. They use an empowered management style built on purpose, guided by values and permeated with trust.

The rest of the organizations rely on two top-down leadership styles in what the report refers to as;

1) "Informed Acquiescence" (62% of organizations), characterized by strict process adherence, decision-making hierarchy, micromanagement and a focus on motivating employees through stick and carrot reward systems; and
2) "Blind Obedience" (30%), a harsher command-and-control management style that relies heavily on coercion, bullying, favoritism, and conformance.

And while only one in 12 organizations used an empowered management style, it was found that the self-governing organizations out-performed their top-down competitors on all 14 performance outcomes evaluated by the study, including levels of resilience, employee loyalty, customer satisfaction and financial performance.

Surprisingly, many organizations seem reluctant to abandon the top-down approaches in favor of a model that better harnesses the potential of people. The good news for employees (and the bad news for those who refuse to empower their workforce) is that the number of companies incorporating a more enlightened approach has almost tripled in just five years.

After I had written the first draft of this book and before I had come across the above report, I wondered whether the example in the Introduction might be outdated since it came from the 1990's. Perhaps organizations had become kinder, gentler "self-governing" places and my cynicism simply prevented me from seeing it?

Then I ran into a neighbor of mine. A highly skilled engineer working on a large project team. So, I asked him how the project was going. His response was straight out of my 1990's experience; he hated it.

He had a project manager who was a bully that liked to scream and intimidate people to get more work done. The work environment was toxic and lacked any sense of collaboration or commitment. People were simply showing up and keeping their heads down to avoid the wrath of the leadership team.

Although not ready for retirement, he wanted out and was hoping to switch jobs, willingly taking less pay or a lesser role within another organization, ideally in an entirely different industry. Although his career had been filled with many similar experiences, either the jobs were getting worse or his tolerance was getting less. He no longer felt proud of his work and he knew if he didn't make a change soon, he'd end up retiring in another ten years feeling empty and dissatisfied with his career.

An ongoing study[2], completed by the Employee Benefit Research Institute (ebri.org), between 1998 and 2012, found that more than half of all employees reported being "moderately satisfied" (40.9%) or "not satisfied at all" (10.5%). What is even more interesting is that the number of people who reported "very satisfied" has dropped by almost 20% over the 14-year span of the report.

Isn't that sad? More than half of workers, many of whom were professionals such as the engineer I spoke with, really had not enjoyed their careers. And the number one reason for that dissatisfaction was due to a lack of respect and appreciation by their employers.

These are people who lived through the "good old days" when companies supposedly took care of you and many employees stayed with a single employer for most their career. They dutifully did what they were told, and they didn't question authority.

Another friend, who worked as a healthcare professional, was being bullied at work several years ago, so she went to the human resources department to report the behavior only to be told a few weeks later that the organization could not guarantee her safety at work and for that reason, she was let go.

Unbelievable!

I can't imagine getting bullied at work, reporting the incidents and then rather than dealing with the problem, they fire you for reporting it! She ended up suing for wrongful dismissal and won but can't talk about it because of a gag order that came with the settlement. Talk about a lack of accountability! The memories of that incident still bring tears to her eyes today.

In 2016, Calgary City Councilor Diane Colley-Urquhart, who sits on the Calgary Police Services (CPS) commission, called out the force for failing to address and improve a culture of bullying, harassment, intimidation and retaliation that had been highlighted in a 2013 internal workplace review[3]. The report noted how such behavior left the people on the receiving end "feeling attacked, angry, isolated frustrated and unsupported." It also noted that in most cases, the affected person did not bring their concerns forward due to fear of intimidation and retaliation.

In response to Colley-Urquhart's statements, Deputy Chief Roger Chaffin noted that many of the recommendations from that report had been implemented and that he could only act on complaints if they were formally received.

If the recommendations have been implemented and there has been no impact, who is accountable? Who is actively reviewing the implementation and identifying obstacles to achieving the intended outcomes? And how can an organizational leader as important as the Chief of Police say he must turn a blind eye to disempowering, disrespectful and possibly even illegal acts in his organization unless someone is willing to raise a formal complaint?

The report specifically points to the "Old Boys Network" found in these male-dominated organizations, with allegations of favoritism, suppression of ideas and suggestions, and the 'bribe, promise and threat' processes used to get ahead or avoid accountability by overlooking, tolerating and rewarding bad behavior.

Civilian and sworn members, both male and female called for the creation of a self-governing culture, based on respect and inclusion. The wanted to see more autonomy in decision-making, appropriate dispute resolution mechanisms, an increase in organizational transparency and trust, and the exploration of ways to promote accountability for behavior in the workplace. It stressed the importance of considering a shift from traditional "command and control" management to a more customer service-based approach. The Deputy Chief recognized that the real issue was culture, "How to become a much more trusted place?"

The latest press releases indicate that implementation of policies to fix the problems at the CPS are now behind schedule and morale on the force has hit an all-time low. Deputy Chief Chaffin blames the morale on the demands he's placing on officers, current workloads, and budget cuts. So, he's asking for more money, more boots on the ground and a willingness of the rank and file to suck it up and do what must be done "in order to embolden public trust and confidence."

He seems to believe that there is an inverse relationship between public trust and employee morale. That's ridiculous. That is unless the leadership at the CPS think that the way to get more from their existing force is to kick them harder and create yet more bureaucracy, attempting to control, rather than inspire their workforce. Sadly, this is the preferred management style for many top-down organizations.

Sexual harassment, bullying, retaliation, intimidation and low morale seem to be a common thread running across Canada's military and police forces. The Royal Canadian Mounted Police (RCMP) recently settled two class action lawsuits to the tune of $100M for bullying and sexual harassment in the workplace. A similar lawsuit is currently proceeding against the Canadian military.

While heading to a writing retreat to finish this book, I was pulled over for speeding by a police officer. He asked where I was going so I told him I was off to a camp to get some solitude and finish writing my book on accountability. He was intrigued. I told him more and when done, he handed me a business card (with the speeding ticket) and told me he'd be interested in reading the book. "Our force has a real internal accountability problem," he assured me. "Can you send me a copy of the book when it's done?" Awesome, one book sold but he's going to be surprised when the invoice comes for $130!

A chaotic, mean-spirited, top-down management style is certainly not limited to the police or military organizations. I just wrapped up a project management assignment where I was bullied, belittled and berated almost from the day I arrived.

Week 1: I was thrown into cost estimating, which I was told was not part of the role. Existing estimates were disorganized and difficult if not impossible to understand. Dozens of equipment and labor rate sheets existed but it I didn't know which was the current pricing that we were using on estimates and no one could tell me. Despite the challenges, in 3 days, I completed estimates for $350,000 worth of work and was criticized for taking too long.

Week 2: I discovered that they had been paying their employees overtime (1.5 times regular pay) to meet additional work requests from our client, but we weren't passing on the overtime cost to that client, creating a loss of over $10,000/month. When I highlighted this issue, I was accused of throwing the entire financial management system into chaos and told that it was my fault that the company was losing that money. "Our financial systems have never been in worse shape!" he accused.

Week 3: I was asked to review one of the owner's estimates and I identified over $600,000 of missing scope. Rather than being shown appreciation for catching the misses, I was yelled at for not knowing where my files were and how to access information at a moment's notice. Did I mention the files were a disaster with no structure or organization?

Week 4: I was lectured for not knowing the detailed costs, the daily spends, the profitability and forecasts for each of my jobs despite him never having such reports from any of my recent predecessors (did I mention I was the 3rd Project Manager in 3 months?), or even have access to the information necessary to produce them.

Week 5: I was fired because I had "added absolutely no value whatsoever".

What an asshole!

My boss was a mean-spirited micromanager who created chaos and then bullied and intimidated people into a state of uselessness until they lived up to the low expectation.

Sadly, I have had far too many of these managers throughout my career (okay this guy was exceptional!) and as a result, I have not lived up to my potential. Most of the organizations I have worked for, struggle with mediocrity and poor performance. The construction contractor above has two current lawsuits against them and a million dollar claim on its current contract and Chrysler closed the Pillette Road plant two years after I quit, laying off over 600 employees.

I tried to make a difference but my initiatives were treated with disdain and suspicion. I was fired by the construction company and time will tell if it survives. And I quit Chrysler, realizing that the leadership was unwilling to challenge the status quo. But if your only option is to quit, or push so hard that you get fired, then complacency and complicity may seem like the only options.

Increasingly, if you are not willing to stand up to the people in your organization who limit individual contributions rather than inspire them to contribute in a bigger way, then don't be surprised when your organization can no longer compete, and you find yourself out of a job or shutting down your business.

I encourage you to use **Accountable** to stimulate conversation, to gain common ground and to make a commitment to creating the structure, supports, and systems to empower people, drive results and maximize impact.

4. The Root of the Problem: Accountability

> *"We all seem to know there is a problem, but have been calling it by different names for years; empowerment, trust, execution, personality styles, conversations, habits, etc. All of these have their roots in how accountability is addressed, but few are nailing the real problem: fixing accountability."*
>
> - Roger Connors & Tom Smith, et al
> Authors of Fixit; Getting Accountability Right

I have always been an organizer and a fixer; someone who could see how things were or weren't working and then come up with ways to make them work better. Whether it was reorganizing my sister-in-law, Deb's kitchen (epic failure) or setting up a tool control program for a manufacturing assembly line (total success), I have always had an eye and ear for spotting chaos then making changes to take the chaos away.

Sadly, most organizations are a lot like my sister-in-law, who insist that there is nothing wrong with the way things are organized and that I should keep my helpful ways to myself. But unlike my sister-in-law, most organizations aren't that nice with the feedback when you start fixing their stuff.

I had one manager yell at me, "I didn't hire you to fix things around here, that's my job!" The sad part was, she was doing a bad job of fixing things and the problems kept piling up and creating an exponential growth in frustration and a significant loss of productivity.

Many organizations seem to have just accepted that they have too many problems that are too deeply embedded in the culture and can never be fixed. But I have always believed I could fix anything; that somewhere below the symptoms and the signals were the root causes of a problem. And if I can get to that root cause, I can fix the problem.

When I was a young engineer, I remember coming to the realization that a lack of competency could easily be the root of many organizational problems. I was fresh out of university and working as a Maintenance Engineer in a steering wheel manufacturing plant. We were having problems with a machine blowing hydraulic pumps and the lead engineer pulled out the hydraulic schematics for the machine and started discussing the issues and observations while pointing at the various symbols on the drawing.

I was dumbfounded, I had never seen a hydraulic schematic before despite five years of engineering school and their discussion was like listening to another language. They turned to me and asked what I thought; I slunk into the corner in embarrassment.

Right then I realized that one of the biggest challenges to workplace success was competency...the workforce's ability to do their jobs. My example demonstrates how the education system wasn't giving graduates the transferable skills they would need to succeed in the workplace and employers were cutting back training programs to reduce costs and focus only on compliance requirements, such as safety training. That left most of us to try to figure things out on our own.

In the early 2000’s, technology was opening up opportunities to revolutionize learning, so I went back to university to do a master's degree in distributed learning (think education and technology), where I focused on empowering learners by enabling informal learning, which is how we learn most of what we know, the creation of peer-to-peer learning networks, and the use of technology to connect those with skill and knowledge to those that need it.

Working for various Canadian colleges, I was able to deliver hands-on, competency-based training for hundreds of people developing real skills critical to the success of their employers. Our computer-based training was delivered to thousands of learners around the world, developing foundational knowledge on which skills could flourish. And I developed job aids for just in time training and support.

During that time, I also recognized that investments in competency training often didn't translate into better results. There seemed to be other forces at play that prevented improved competency from having the impact you might expect.

A few years later, I moved into an Operational Excellence (OE) role at a large engineering design and construction firm. They liked my background in both engineering and education and offered me an amazing opportunity to expand my base of knowledge and experience from competency to the creation of high-performance teams. My job was to apply a variety of principles, systems, and tools for sustainable organizational improvement.

I was assigned as OE Lead for a large project team with over 1000 engineers, designers, and administrative staff. When I began working with the teams I made two immediate observations,

1. There was a high degree of confusion around who was responsible for what, who could approve what, how the processes worked and where things could be found.
2. There was no compelling sense of team or vision of success, departments were highly siloed and clients were the enemy.

My solution was to first develop clarity through the creation of tools like process maps, responsibility matrices, and user-friendly work instructions. I ran workshops to define scope limits and interfaces while gaining alignment on responsibilities. I would then overlay this work with a team methodology to instill a sense of collaboration, respect, and organizational pride.

I had many successes during this time but found that the clarity tools only worked when a committed manager enforced the rules and respected individual responsibilities. And if people couldn't speak up when the rules were being broken, then the team development concepts were lost due to a lack of trust.

No matter how much structure, support and vision we provided the team, there was always a small group of micromanagers, bullies, and heroes that felt the rules did not apply to them; that the processes were designed for people who didn't understand how to get things done; and that decision-making authority was given to tenure and position, not to the tasks that people carried out. And those acts of defiance by that small, yet influential group quickly empowered others to retreat to the status quo as well.

If I had clarity of process and individual responsibilities, competent and confident workers, and a high-performance team structure that could support higher levels of collaboration and commitment, then why was it that the heroes, bullies, and micromanagers could still hold people down and prevent them from being the best they could be. It proved that lack of process, alignment and collaboration are a problem but not the root of the problem. Similarly, bullying, heroism, and micromanagement were also not the primary issues. These cultural challenges were simply barriers to the real root cause; a lack of accountability.

Micromanagers will dictate decisions if they believe they are the ones who will be punished if things go wrong, and likely they are right in the top-down business world. The problem is, they often don't understand the complexity of the situation or the needs of the customer or stakeholders and end up dictating self-serving solutions that create chaos and add little value for anyone other than themselves and their boss. The person carrying out the work simply does what they are told, even if that work has negative impacts on other stakeholders. Then when bad things happen, the micromanager says, "I thought he was smarter! Why would he have done that?"

The cultural barriers that enable micromanagement, bullying and heroism take accountability away from front-line workers and don't necessarily pass them on to the managers who are dictating decisions from afar. When the dust settled on the 2013 BP Deepwater Horizon offshore oil well disaster, no one was held accountable, yet every individual along the chain of events made significant compromises in meeting stakeholder needs and expectations.

Upper management used intimidation and coercion to get people to bypass processes, using directives like, "You get it done or we will get someone else in here who will!" Micromanagers disrespected and overrode front-line decision-making and workers became increasingly disengaged. And when the preventable disaster hit, those workers lacked competency in the heat of the moment and failed to execute proper emergency procedures.

With an accountable culture, the Deepwater Horizon disaster would have never happened because the mistakes that were being made at every level in the organization would have been corrected at their source, rather than those mistakes growing and transferring through the organization; festering and morphing into increasingly critical errors.

Moving to a culture of accountability is the single biggest decision an organization can make to improve their performance. And fortunately, it's likely the easiest change because most of your people will support the transformation. People want more from their jobs! They want to contribute at a higher level, not to overshadow their managers but to contribute in the biggest way possible.

Aligning decision-making authority with task authority and holding each individual accountable for their work allows your people to be the best they can and to contribute to your organization in a more meaningful way. It is the win–win that organizations have been ignoring for too long.

5. Accountability: The Leading Indicator of Success

> *"Accountability is meeting or exceeding the needs and expectations of our customers and stakeholders"*
>
> *Pete Myers*
> *Author - Accountable*

Throughout the book, I refer to a lack of accountability as a root cause of most organizational challenges. So it only stands to reason that accountability is a powerful leading indicator of organizational success. That's a pretty bold and potentially transformational statement, so I wanted to expand on it to help you to see what I see; if you can improve the quality of the interactions between people on your team, you will improve your results.

Figure 1: A Typical Process

To understand leading indicators, it's important to understand processes. Processes are a series of tasks or activities that transform inputs to outputs that serve a specific function. The process to make ice cream includes the process of mixing inputs of milk and cream and freezing for four hours, resulting in an output of ice cream. Any variation in the quality of the milk or cream or the freezing time or temperature will affect the quality of the ice cream. It only makes sense.

To have a high-performance process with consistent quality outputs, it is then critical that you have;

- an in-control process and
- consistent, repeatable inputs.

If the inputs do not meet your needs and expectations, then you must have the ability to reject the inputs and possibly shut down the process until acceptable inputs have been provided. Sadly, that ability to reject bad inputs is often missing in our organizations and we are somehow expected to still produce acceptable outputs, even though our inputs are defective. As the owner of the ice cream process, you are the customer of the milk and cream. If the milk is sour and you are forced to use it anyhow, how good do you think the ice cream is going to be?

Most people who have worked in Quality or Information Technology (IT) are familiar with the expression, "Garbage In; Garbage Out". Regardless of how in-control or robust your process may be, the introduction of bad inputs will produce bad outputs. If, however, you have an in-control process and your inputs are consistently within the tolerances that you require, the outputs will meet or exceed customers and stakeholders needs and expectations.

One of the fundamental breakdowns in the top-down management model is its inability to empower the worker to reject inputs if they do not meet their quality requirements. When I worked for Chrysler, people on the line were not allowed to stop it if their parts were defective. They were told to install the parts and the problem would be fixed later.

But at Toyota, they understood that it was the responsibility of each member of the team to stop the line if they were given defective parts rather than simply installing them and letting someone else fix the problem later. They knew the importance of stopping the spread of the quality virus, where their North American counterparts would go ahead and produce defective vehicles then rework them in the yard without ever stopping the line. Problem is, a lot of the defects that went into our repair yard ended up being defects in many people's driveways.

The second key understanding is the importance of an in-control process. An in-control process is a statistical term which refers to a process that has a consistent normal distribution with predictable, repeatable and symmetrical results about a vertical axis.

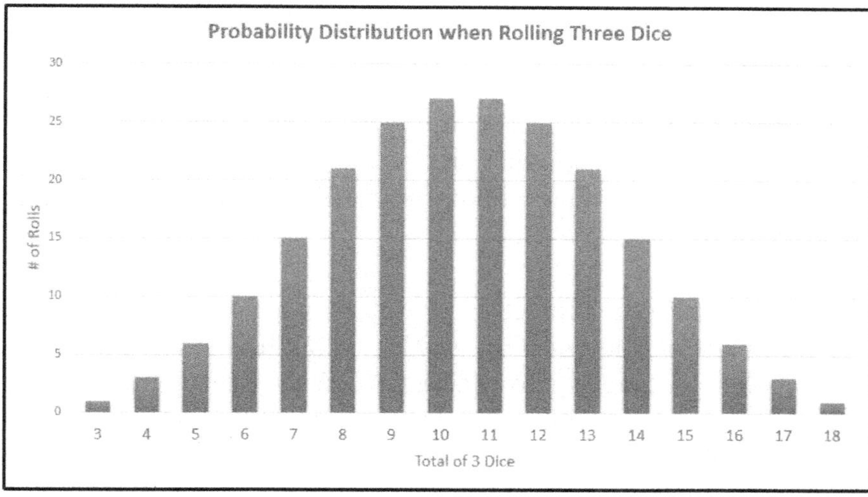

Figure 2: A Normal Distribution

Many organizations try to fix their problems by implementing six sigma quality initiatives, but their processes are not in-control (predictable and repeatable) and you can't incrementally fix something that is highly unpredictable, you must first get it in-control.

Once you have consistent inputs and an in-control process, then you can begin to focus on continuous improvement methodologies with the intention of monitoring variation through the identification of key variables or indicators. There are two types of indicators you can identify;

1) Leading Indicators
2) Lagging Indicators

Leading indicators are typically focused on the quality of the inputs to a process or an actual variable of the process, whereas lagging indicators usually measure outputs from the process.

Lagging indicators are more common as they are easier to measure, but they are often difficult to improve or influence and can take hours, months or even years to see the impact of changes to inputs or processes. Leading indicators, on the other hand, can be harder to measure but easier to improve or influence. By better controlling the inputs and the process, you can avoid and eliminate the cost and chaos associated with trying to fix the downstream quality issue.

Typical lagging indicators used by corporations include Customer Satisfaction, Net Profit, EBITA or Return on Investment. These and others are all important measures of performance but can't tell us whether the improvements that are implemented today will have an impact on the bottom line without a significant lag after the initial investment was made.

When I worked as a Project Engineer, overseeing the design and construction of plastic injection molds, I often had to test out a new tooling before putting it into production. We relied on suppliers to monitor the quality of their inputs to our plastic molding process and insisted they provide documentation to prove as much.

We would then begin running the tooling adjusting one variable at a time to determine how large (or small) the variation was for acceptable parts. Our goal was not to make as many good parts as possible; it was to make as many bad parts as possible by changing the process parameters and developing correlations between good quality products and acceptable parameter limits.

We called this defining the window of operation or process optimization. If I could find a parameter with a direct correlation to part quality, say hydraulic pressure, then I could find the limits of acceptable hydraulic pressure (window of operation) and then monitor it as a leading indicator of success, resulting in a high degree of confidence that the finished parts would be within their allowable tolerance range. This ability to move upstream has a direct impact on the consistency of the finished product and the profitability of the job.

Business leaders are always looking for upstream, leading indicators that will tell them sooner whether their investments have been worthwhile, but indicators such as profitability or customer satisfaction are lagging indicators with significant delays in determining whether an investment had the desired impact.

Customer Loyalty is forward-looking (will they buy again?) but it is still a lagging indicator which cannot be determined until an order has been shipped. Accountability measures the quality of the interactions between team members right from the beginning of any sales or services process. Remember, accountability is defined as

> "Meeting or exceeding customer and
> stakeholder needs and expectations"

If your Business Development group does a poor job scoping project requirements, it will be difficult for the project team to be successful. If I prepare a report, with false or misleading information, my customer, who is often my boss, must rely on that report to make decisions. Without good information, my boss is going to make bad decisions that manifest errors into a loss of value.

By adopting a more accountable workplace, the cost of transactions declines as errors or omissions disappear. That drives cost savings, schedule confidence, satisfied stakeholders, and results.

Before undertaking a journey of accountability, organizations must be realistic about how willing they are to make changes to their culture to unleash the power of everyone.

- Can you align decision-making authority with task authority?
- Are you willing to do the work required to create clarity?
- To ensure competency?
- To communicate effectively?
- To gain commitment?
- To work collaboratively?

And do you have the authority and the willingness to enforce consequences if needs and expectations are not being met?

If you are not willing to change, you could be in for some tough times ahead. Studies are showing that organizations with a more inspired and empowered workforce are significantly outperforming their top-down competitors. In an increasingly connected and competitive global market, can your organization afford to keep making mistakes and incurring unnecessary costs?

6. Why Change Now?

> *"The world is not just rapidly changing, it's being dramatically reshaped – it operates differently."*
>
> \- Dov Seidman
> Founder & CEO, LRN
> Author of "Why HOW We Do Anything Means Everything"

There are many indicators that tell us that the age of the Old Boys Network and the command and control organization is increasingly failing its shareholders and society. Old school incumbents are being overthrown by upstarts, who promote collaboration and commitment to values.

These disruptors then drive higher levels of customer satisfaction which in turn increase expectations of consumers, who then push those expectations on the traditional organizations. But increased expectations require higher levels of agility, innovation, and communication not realized in top-down organizations.

Before I get too carried away, it's important to note that the "Top-down" or "Command and Control" management model has been the dominant business model since the beginning of human history. And to even ponder the possibilities of a world without this approach to how we get things down should be questioned. Is **Accountable** simply the musings of a frustrated worker who wants to break free from the yoke of his oppressors?

Or are my feelings of oppression simply a lack of appreciation of how good I really have it? After all, look at all the good things we have in our lives today? The total net worth of the average household has gone up dramatically since World War II (see Figure 3).

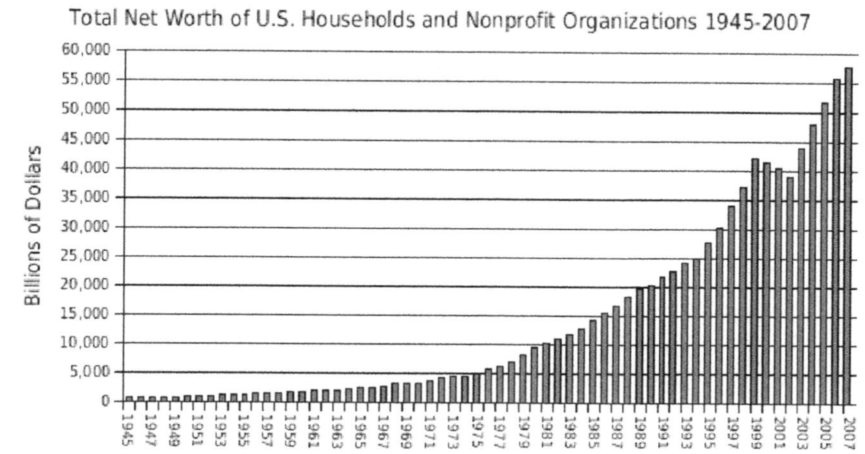

Figure 3: Total Net Worth of Households and Nonprofits[4]

I can travel anywhere (almost) in the world simply by showing my passport and jumping on a plane. The freedom of movement that our society has today is unprecedented in history.

Civil rights have vastly improved in the last century and women's rights are moving the needle. Admittedly, there are still many battlegrounds on this front, but in my lifetime, which is a blink of the eye on the human scale, everything has changed.

Our healthcare system is helping us live longer. Since I was born in 1961, the average Canadian's life expectancy at birth has increased by ten years. That doesn't even speak to the incredible feats that can be achieved by our health care system, like my hip replacement a few years ago.

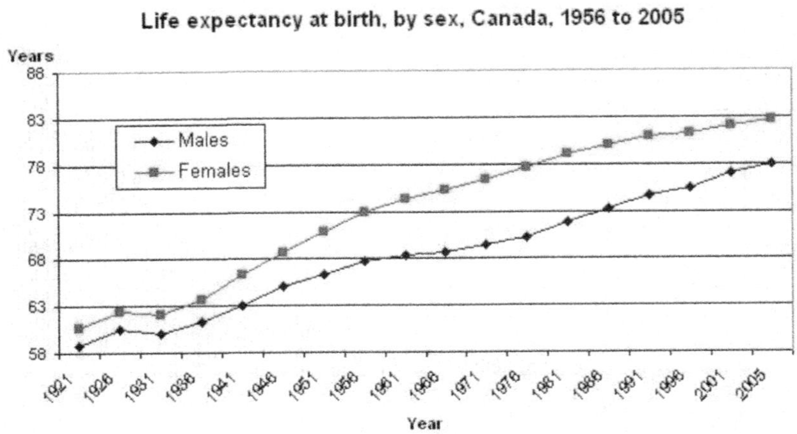

Figure 4: Life Expectancy by Sex at Birth[5]

Facilitated by an explosion in technology, adults often have a more active lifestyle than their parents. I am 56 years old and I still ski, mountain bike and play hockey. My parents stopped being active once they had children. Extreme sports wouldn't even exist if we didn't have the health care system to fix all the dislocations, fractures and tears that our sports addictions produce.

Rather than look at these dramatic changes as a reason to simply be appreciative of how good things are, they provide me with an even greater urgency to change. Will we lose our society and our way of life if we are not willing to change to a more progressive, people-centric management style? Not if our workplaces, governments and non-profit organizations continue to be as successful in the future as they have been in the past.

But there are clear signs that past performance is not an indicator of future results. Here are a few reasons why;

The Operating System Has Hit Its Limit

Regardless of what industry you are in, your work has become exponentially more complex in the last 20 years. Whether you consider safety and regulatory requirements, globalization, use of technology, meeting stakeholder needs, or additional reporting requirements, life is not nearly as simple as it was only a generation ago.

That complexity seems to be creating a tipping point where our traditional management models are stalling out. Many veterans in my industry agree that things are worse than they can ever remember. More chaotic. More confused. More mean-spirited than ever before.

The researchers at LRN refer to this limitation in the HOW Report as a limitation of an organization's "Operating System" (OS). Their study confirms the poor performance of the command and control operating system (ccOS) and the top-down operating system (tdOS), are being bogged down by their inefficient and ineffective processes.

Fixing the bad OS is not about adding more RAM, another hard drive or even replacing the motherboard. It's replacing the OS with one that talks, walks and thinks differently. They call it the "Human Operating System" (hOS), one that relies on the interpretive and analytical skills of people to drive higher levels of performance and success.

If the ccOS and tdOS are getting bogged down, there must be signs or symptoms (eg: noises or overheating) that would help to make that determination, and I believe they are abundant and compelling.

Studies conducted by Christine Porath, Associate Professor of Management at Georgetown University and author of Mastering Civility, a Manifesto for the Workplace[6], show that workplace incivility has increased by 13% since 1998 and sits at an all-time high, with 62% of employees being treated rudely by colleagues at least once a month. Similarly, employee satisfaction and engagement are at an all-time low despite countless investments by organizations to rid their organizations of this culture?

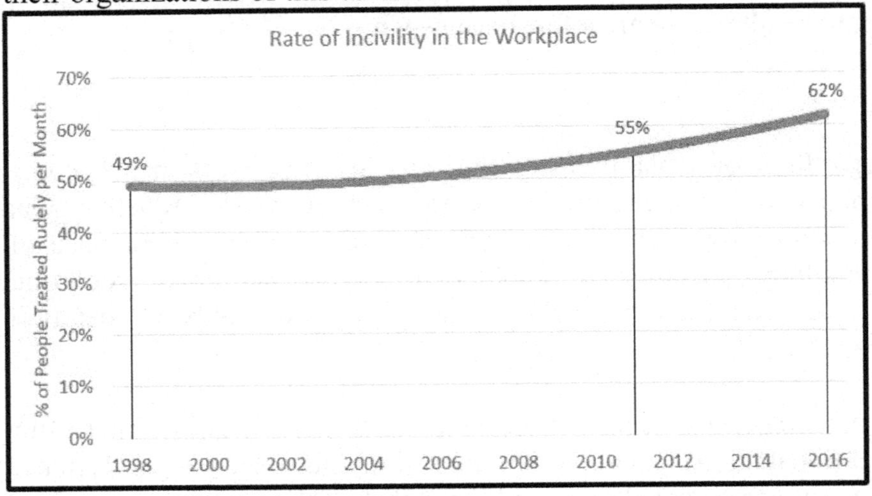

Figure 5: Workplace Incivility on the Rise[6]

This is all despite increases in organizational spending on everything from inclusion workshops to communication technology to team building activities, even accountability training can't seem to solve the problem. All too often these "feel good" activities don't have a lasting impact and are simply undermined to maintain the status quo.

Sadly, ccOS's (30% of organizations in 2016) and tdOS's (62%) demand little more than compliance and achieve nothing more than mediocrity. The hOS's (8%), however, inspire elevated behaviors of courage, compassion, and creativity. They turn chaos into clarity, competition into collaboration and compliance into accountability.

Another common indicator suggesting that our society needs to move away from the top-down management model is worker engagement. A quick search of the internet will turn up endless statistics and advice on the seriousness of the worker engagement problem with possibly a loss of over $7 trillion worldwide...ANNUALLY. Only 15% of Canadian workers are considered engaged with the remaining either disengaged (67%); people who are there in body only, or actively disengaged (18%); people who willingly take value away through sabotage, theft, neglect, and negligence.

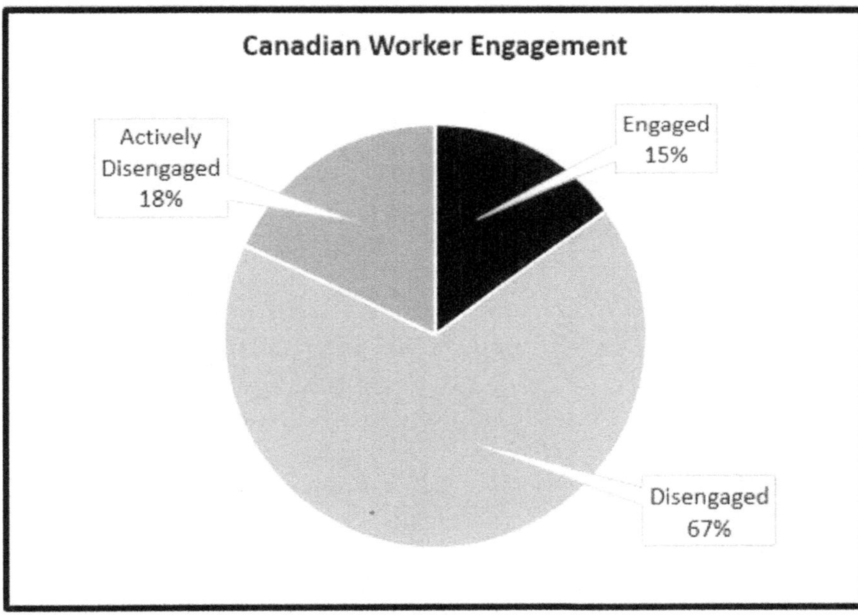

Figure 6: Canadian Worker Disengagement[7]

And if you think engagement scores are bad, it is important to understand that engagement is the minimum that you want from your employees. Engaged employees may ensure tasks are done to the identified requirements, but they often don't have a strong understanding of WHY they are doing the work or are willing to go the extra mile to meet commitments.

Without a clear understanding of customers and stakeholders needs, it is difficult, even for an engaged employee, to understand if work being done is going to serve the purpose required.

To get the highest levels of performance, employees and volunteers must not only be engaged but also inspired with a strong sense of direction and pride and by opportunities for meaningful personal and professional growth. And inspired by working relationships infused with a shared sense of purpose. The old OS doesn't believe it's their job to inspire! "That's what your paycheck is for!" they'd insist.

Sadly, paychecks do little to inspire.

The next reason has to do with some scientific research that was carried out in the 1940's by Abraham Maslow. In his paper "A Theory of Human Motivation". Maslow's theory suggests that the most basic level of needs must be met before the individual will strongly desire (or focus motivation upon) the secondary or higher-level needs. He identified the most basic need as Physiological, the need for human survival.

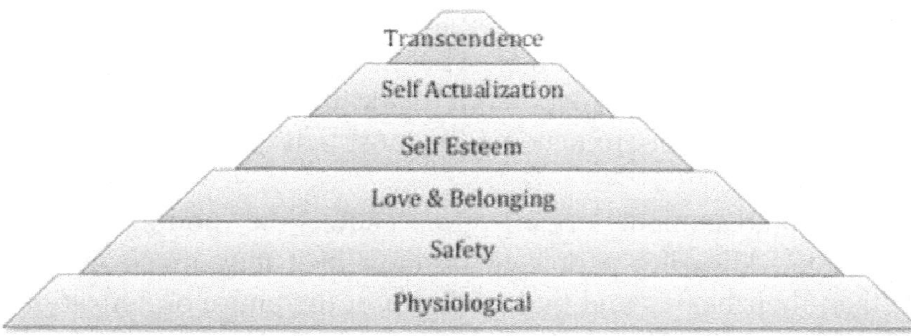

Figure 7: Maslow's Hierarchy of Needs

Once those needs were satisfied, humans moved up the hierarchy of needs to Safety - including personal and financial well-being. They established cultures where war was no longer a factor, began building police forces to ensure public safety, created jobs to drive economic security, and expanded health care to ensure personal well-being.

With the scars of World War II still fresh in the minds of my parent's generation, yet Safety still firmly entrenched in North America, that generation moved up to the need for Love and Belonging. The 40-hour work week started to become the norm, allowing people to have free time to pursue team sports or join a charitable organization like Rotary, Shriners or the Kinsmen, which my dad belonged to.

They appreciated the opportunities that life was beginning to provide outside the workplace and they were satisfied to just have a job with decent pay. That fueled the middle-class boom of the 1950's to 70's.

When I started work in the mid-eighties, young graduates were looking for careers that allowed the pursuit of self-esteem and the ability to express themselves. Building personal competency became increasingly important and the notion of respect not just up the org chart, but across the entire organization was being instilled.

By the 2000's, companies were creating values statements and trying to shift the workforce to a more respectful, team-based approach. Flexible work hours, working from home and casual dress codes all became the norm to meet the increasing need to express oneself.

Today's graduates continue up the hierarchy to a state of self-actualization. We are already seeing this in the IT sector and we have seen it in sports for quite a while. This level refers to the need for a person to achieve their full potential. It's the desire to accomplish everything that one can, to become the most that one can be.

Top-down management organizations shun the notion of self-actualization. Allowing people to be their best may mean they are better than their bosses and that could upset the entire organizational structure. In command and control, the goal is to keep everyone the same. Yet in the world of self-actualization, everyone wants to contribute in a unique way.

Managing in the world of self-actualization is tough. Sweeping policies that attempt to limit human influence over outcomes, rather than tap into their people's potential, risk chasing self-actualizers to the exits of your organization.

Companies that are going to be successful at attracting the changing expectations of employees will create inviting cultures that enable freedom of expression and inspiration for each employee or volunteer to contribute their full character and creativity in pursuit of a shared purpose.

Going back to Maslow's Hierarchy of Needs, there is a sixth level shown at the top of the illustration. Elite athletes and executives increasingly are moving to an even higher form of self-actualization...team actualization (Maslow calls this Transcendence).

This ultimate state of being is achieved when we help others achieve their self-actualization and working together as a team, achieve amazing results. Any great athlete will quickly tell you that the personal accolades were nice, but the best memories and greatest satisfaction come from contributing to the success of a championship team and that championship ring has more meaning than all the individual trophies and accolades combined.

Visionary CEO's are increasingly tearing down barriers to workplace accountability by creating cultures that allow their workers to be their best; to be more innovative; to be more productive and; to be safer.

They realize that to achieve their own dreams and aspirations, they must maximize their investments in their team and they must create the tools, systems, and processes necessary to ensure mistakes don't prevent the organization from achieving its full potential. Looking back, that retired CEO will take the greatest sense of pride for being the leader of a great team that made a difference.

Most important it's about PERFORMANCE. The HOW report[1] found that organizations identified as "Self-Governing" outperformed their top-down counterparts on every key indicator of organizational success, including market share, customer satisfaction, innovation, employee engagement, and performance sustainability with lower levels of misconduct.

The report defines "Self-Governing" (SG) as organizations that are values-based, purpose-inspired and that empower their employees (or volunteers) to contribute in the largest way possible. And the numbers are impressive;

17% improvement over organizations which classify as Informed Acquiescence (AI) = heavily process driven, hierarchy-based, with a top-down, micromanagement style; and

57% over Blind Obedience (BO) organizations - power-based, task driven, and use a heavy-handed command and control management style.

In the study they found six key findings[1];

1) Self-Governing organizations are increasing (from 3% in 2012 to 8% in 2016) and Blind Obedience organizations are decreasing (43% in 2012 to 30% in 2016).
2) Self-Governing organizations out-perform because their people out-perform, with 97% of employees operating at a high-performance level compared to 80% at Informed Acquiescence organizations and only 36% at Blind Obedience organizations.
3) Leaders who emphasize shaping character and fostering freedom are more effective leaders and are three times more likely to deliver high business performance.
4) The culture in the C Suite does not reflect the culture within the organization with respect to trust, collaboration and information sharing.
5) The key enabler of innovation is trust, with eleven times greater innovation than low trust organizations. By the way,

government agencies score lowest on trust surveys (~3%), dramatically lower than any other industry (15 – 48%).

6) Inspiration drives impact on performance beyond engagement. Employees who are authentically dedicated, purpose-driven and deeply accountable are 27% more predictive of organizational success than an engaged employee.

The top-down management model is increasingly showing lower returns and is not what today's graduates are looking for. They seek a new model which empowers them and allows them to be the best they can be. They seek to work in a state of transparency and clarity. And they seek to be collaborative and accountable for the work they do.

Unfortunately, the top-down management leaders continue to defend their model, despite their challenges of getting work done, being profitable and attracting young graduates. Rather than be open to change, they push on governments to allow more temporary foreign workers into the country, workers who reside lower on the hierarchy of needs and will put up with bad managers and chaotic workplaces.

I am not slamming immigrants here, but I don't believe the top-down management model is sustainable in developed countries, where the workplace has gotten dramatically more complex; where people are now seeking jobs that allow them to be their best; and where Self-Governing competitors are out-performing them on every measure of success.

If we don't change, we might all find ourselves out of work.

7. The Quest for Accountability

> *"When it comes to privacy and accountability, people always demand the former for themselves and the latter for everyone else."*
>
> David Brin
> Scientist and Author

A former manager of mine at a large oil and gas company, once told me, "A lack of accountability is not necessarily a bad thing."

And in a command and control environment, he was right. The last thing you want to be in a top-down organization is accountable. You might as well call yourself the scapegoat. However, accountability is what people need to drive higher levels of personal satisfaction and organizations need to drive higher levels of success.

To drive higher levels of accountability, an organization must rise above mediocrity and nurture elevated behaviors of courage, compassion, and creativity, to gain the resilience, agility and performance needed in a global, ever-changing economy.

However, to get into a sane conversation about accountability we need to head off the people who will say things like:

> "When you strip away the decision-making authority from responsibility, it becomes accountability."

My response is, when you strip decision-making authority from responsibility, it becomes chaos, disengagement, and micromanagement.

Or how about this one:

> "You can delegate responsibility, but you can't delegate accountability"

If you delegate responsibility, you have delegated accountability, but that doesn't mean you're not accountable too. If the person to whom I delegate fails, odds are, I will also fail. This is where we get into problems with micromanagement. It seems there are only two options; blindly trust that your workers will be successful and let them do their job, or micromanage and make all the decisions and set all the priorities to ensure they don't fail. Sadly, they still do. There is a third option, hold them accountable for the work they do.

To really understand accountability and to get value from it, we must be open to a new way of defining it.

The dictionary defines accountable as;

> *ac·count·able*
>
> 1 : LIABLE <accountable for the burglary>
> 2 : obliged to accept responsibility

Interestingly, accountable uses the term responsible in its definition, that then makes it a synonym. A synonym is a word or phrase that means exactly or nearly the same as another word or phrase in the same language. So, let's look at the definition of responsible;

> *re·spon·si·ble*
>
> 1 a : liable to be called on to answer b : liable to be called to account as the primary cause, motive, or agent c : liable to legal review or in case of fault to penalties
> 2 : marked by or involving accountability

Alternatively, responsible uses accountability to define it, and both words use liable in their definition. Accountability and responsibility imply potential liability; being charged in a court of law for neglect or malpractice and going to jail. And that is another reason that accountability is so important and so elusive.

The only difference between responsible and accountable seems to be from a legal perspective; anything can be responsible, only people can be accountable. For example, a failure of a structural member can be responsible for the collapse of a building, but it cannot be accountable. Only a person can be accountable.

Much of our perspective on accountability is tied to this notion of liability; "Who's throat do we choke if things go wrong?". The problem is, we tend to ask, "Who is accountable?" once the shit hits the fan, and that's too late.

Accountability is a much more positive and powerful tool and predictor of success if we ask the question, "To whom are we accountable?" when we are first assigned the task. This gives us the opportunity to get a better understanding of who our customers and stakeholders are, as well as their needs, expectations and concerns in relation to the task being performed. Only once we understand the entire spectrum of needs and expectations can we begin to create solutions that can meet them. There will be no need to choke a single throat if the hundreds of contributing throats are empowered, supported and held accountable for the work that they do.

Figure 8: Accountable Driver

To gain a more valuable understanding of accountability, I often use the following graphic to help validate the concepts. In this example, I tell my class that you have been given responsibility by your boss to drive him and a colleague to a meeting across town. Who is accountable to get the three people to the meeting on time?

It depends! From a client perspective, the boss committed to being on time, so they will hold him accountable. But if the boss delegated the task or the responsibility, he must also delegate the authority and accountability to do the task to the employee. In other words, the driver, not the delegator of the authority is now accountable.

The driver is accountable to the boss and the colleague to get them to the meeting safely and on time. He is also accountable to;

- Other drivers
- Pedestrians
- Cyclists
- Government bodies who set the rules of the road
- Police services, who enforce the rules of the road

But what happens if the boss begins to demand that the driver speed up, possibly run a couple yellow lights to get them there on time? That would be the same as micromanagement. The driver knows the rules of the road, but the boss is trying to influence them using their authority and position of power. And if the driver gets pulled over for speeding, the driver will be accountable, not the boss!

Figure 9: Micromanaging Passenger

In the workplace, the micromanaging boss is not satisfied if the worker does not do what they are told, so they will intervene and begin making decisions for the employee. That would be the equivalent of your boss grabbing the steering wheel while you're driving.

It is now unclear who is accountable for driving. They are both trying to steer the car and no one person is accountable if the car is in an accident. The boss would blame the employee,

> "If you just did what I told you to do, we wouldn't be in this mess!"

And the employee would respond,

> "If you didn't stick your nose into it, this would have never happened!"

This obvious violation of responsibilities and the subsequent impact on accountabilities are clear and now creates a conflict between the driver and the boss. The driver can do one of two things.

1) They can release control of the steering wheel to the boss and begin asking what he should be doing with the brake and gas (notice how the driver relinquishes all responsibilities when one aspect of their task has been subverted), or

2) The driver can land a solid elbow to the boss' chin, rendering him unconscious as the driver wrestles control of the wheel back.

In the workplace, although I have many times wanted to land the elbow, I, like most of you in a similar situation, simply relinquished control, and silently dropped my accountability to my customers and stakeholders. And my experience has been that those who seize control of tasks are not too concerned with meeting many people's needs or expectations other than their own.

But what does a boss do if the person driving the car is incompetent? They are swerving across the centerline and onto the shoulder. They are speeding up to twice the speed limit or crawling doing half the recommended speed?

As a manager, if you feel that someone who you have assigned responsibility to is not going to meet the needs of all customers and stakeholders, then you have a decision to make, you can;

1) Let the inevitable accident happen,

2) Try to seize control of the task but we all know how badly that can go,

3) Use your authority to tell the driver to pull over and take the responsibility away.

The third option is missing in management today. It seems most job descriptions are based on industry norms rather than individual strengths so rather than delegate work to the person who is good at it, we tend to delegate to the person whose job description says they are responsible for the work. And if they are not competent at one thing, we dismiss all their other skills and experience and tend to marginalize or eliminate them all together.

Understanding the relationship between responsibility, accountability, and success is critical, so let me share an example from my work.

I have worked as a Project Manager on many jobs. As the PM, I have overall responsibility and accountability for the project completion. Then I hire an engineer to be my Structural Lead and I delegate the structural design work to them. They now have responsibility and accountability for designing steel structures that meets all requirements and industry codes. And they must make all the decisions necessary to meet that objective while also meeting or exceeding all customer needs and expectations.

When that engineer approves a drawing by applying their engineering stamp, my accountability and therefore my liability stops when I can demonstrate that;

1) They are licensed in the jurisdiction of the project
2) The design followed proper process, including peer review
3) They made or approved all decisions related to the design
4) They weren't coerced or intimidated

As a leader, when I recognize a problem or deficiency, it is my responsibility to lean into the situation and determine what I can do to help drive success. In shifting from command and control to a collaborative work environment, it is critical that we respect individual responsibilities while understanding that the responsibilities of my team support the completion of my own higher-level responsibilities.

Many companies today use RACI charts, with the acronym standing for **R**esponsible **A**ccountable, **C**onsultant and **I**nformed. And much of the confusion around accountability and responsibility comes from this practice. Unfortunately, too many users of the tool think that the methodology allows responsibility to be split from accountability and they will say things like;

"You're responsible but I'm accountable, so you'll do it my way"

But what the **A** in RACI stands for is not Accountable. It stands for the Accountability we have to our customers and stakeholders. Thinking that one person is responsible for the work and another is accountable is a dangerous way of thinking and forms the basis for bullying and micromanagement.

It implies that the accountable person can override the responsible person, so tend to dictate all decisions related to the execution of the work. You will do it, but they will tell you how to do it and when to do it. This highly disempowering approach undermines the responsible person's ability to understand the complexity of the situation and the needs of their stakeholders and customers.

That is exactly what happened on another occasion at Chrysler. As mentioned in the Introduction, we were in a plant shutdown and I was responsible for the technical recommendation for over one million dollars in tooling.

My manager had told me that my recommendations had to be to corporate procurement by first thing Monday morning and I was to order all the tools from one vendor. That vendor was our primary tooling supplier in the plant and had been for years. But more recently, some competitors had edged their way in by offering tools that were lighter and faster especially in certain torque ranges.

By Sunday, I had my spreadsheet completed detailing every job, its torque requirements and a table comparing price, weight, and speed of the incumbent vendor's tools for each application as well as the two competitors. I realized I was accountable to my manager and his directive to only buy from the incumbent supplier, but I was also accountable to the front-line workers and assembly manager for the speed and ergonomics of the final solution. I was okay spending more money to appease my boss (although I questioned whether he was getting a kickback from that supplier and trying to keep their competitors out of the plant), but on three specific applications, the incumbent's tool did not make sense. They were twice as heavy and almost half the speed.

Based on the weight and the position the worker had to be in to do the assembly, their tools were the wrong solution and would result in workplace injuries, lost productivity and potential for a work refusal. I demonstrated the ownership necessary to drive a win-win and I had done my due diligence. I would be able to demonstrate to my manager why I had not followed his one supplier directive. I submitted the order and copied him on it, including the justification spreadsheet.

When I arrived at the plant on Monday morning, my boss was livid and could hardly stand to look at me. Within minutes, the HR department was in his office and not long after that, I sat in a meeting room across from him and two HR representatives. I was being accused of insubordination.

From a legal perspective, the act is not considered insubordination if you are refusing to perform an action that is unethical or illegal or not within the scope of authority of the person issuing the order. Wasn't I responsible for ordering and installing the new tooling so should I have the authority to make the decisions and alter directions based on my front-line knowledge? Or was my boss too busy holding the steering wheel?

Too often, command and control managers believe that their position overrides that of the responsible person if that person is below them on the organization chart. And to challenge or even question that unwritten rule is nothing less than insubordination and must be punished.

Moving decisions up the ladder, away from the people who are closest to and understand the situation the best introduces significant risk of not meeting stakeholder needs and expectations. I see many organizations unknowingly taking this risk. A person, regardless of how smart or experienced they may be, will struggle to understand the complexities and nuances of a project or issue in which they are not embedded and will tend to make simplistic decisions that may meet his or her needs while overlooking the needs of others.

In the case of my manager at Chrysler, he tried to override my accountability to the worker on the line and their safety and to the production leadership for productivity of the line. If I would have just done what my boss told me to do, I would have ignored the needs of my co-workers, the people I support and work with every day.

I lived up to my accountabilities, even when I knew I would be taking a hit from management. I owed it to that worker to give them the best tool possible to do that job and I took my responsibilities and accountabilities to my customers seriously. I wasn't going to let my manager force me to make a bad decision that would likely injure a worker and lower our productivity. Besides, I valued my relationship with the workforce I supported and was not willing to jeopardize that.

Initially, my boss pushed for a one-week suspension with no pay for my act of insubordination, but we were in the middle of a plant shutdown and the Tooling Engineer is critical to its success, so he moved for a one-day suspension with no pay but would allow me to work through it.

Initially, my boss pushed for a one-week suspension with no pay for my act of insubordination, but we were in the middle of a plant shutdown and the Tooling Engineer is critical to its success, so he moved for a one-day suspension with no pay but would allow me to work through it.

I refused so they ended up not suspending me, only putting a nasty letter in my file. In hindsight, I should have accepted the offer to work through my unpaid suspension, I likely would have been eligible for overtime pay as my regular pay had been suspended! (Did I mention that I was a unionized engineer?)

When people use their authority to make your decisions, they strip you of your intrinsic motivation. If you are a good foot soldier, you will do what your leader tells you, even if you know it's not right. If not, you will either simply disengage and take no ownership of the task, or if your rebellious like I am, you will just do it your way and deal with the fallout when it inevitably happens.

And therein lies the biggest challenge to accountability. Too many senior leaders think accountability is about who will be punished. Who will be the one throat to choke if things go wrong? I get this position from a leadership perspective. It states that we will hold our team to be accountable for their work, but we will defend their work as our own. We won't throw anyone under the bus.

In the case of the employee driving his boss to the meeting, if they were late, the boss would have an obligation to take ownership for the tardiness, rather than blame the subordinate who he delegated the driving task to. But as leaders, if we think that we are accountable for other's work, then that means we are responsible and liable for it as well. Are you? Should you be?

Five years after the BP Deepwater Horizon disaster in the Gulf of Mexico, which resulted in the loss of 11 lives and was the largest environmental disaster in human history, US federal prosecutors ended the government's pursuit of criminal charges against two rig supervisors meaning that although several companies share liability, no one will ever spend any time behind bars for the incident.

The US court system was highly criticized for only going after the two frontline supervisors. Critics and court findings showed that BP had a culture of cutting corners and intimidating its workers to compromise standard procedures, regulatory requirements and following necessary timelines to carry out work in a safe manner. It's been reported that workers knew that the Macondo well had serious problems before the blowout ever happened. It had been nicknamed, "the well from hell". But tracking and managing accountability must start before the well

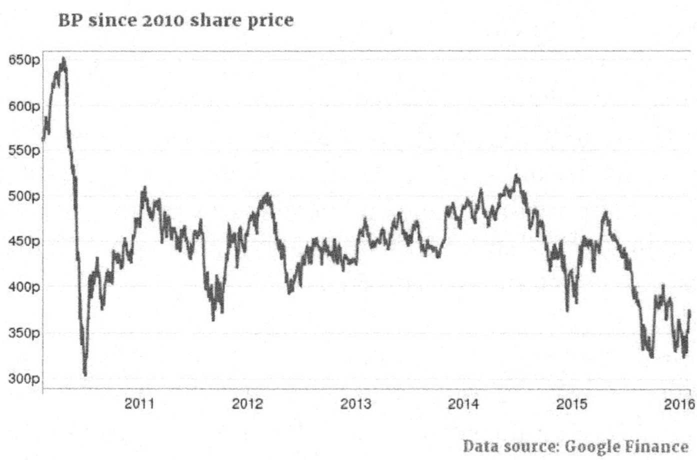

Figure 10: BP share price since the Deepwater Horizon

blows! After the damage is done, accountability can only result in liability, fines, firings or jail time, and that doesn't benefit anyone. In the case of BP, it resulted in over $25B in cleanup costs, fines, and settlements. That doesn't even include the loss of shareholder value when BP stocks plummeted and have never recovered. Does firing a key executive make those shareholders feel better? Maybe, but I think they'd feel a lot better if their personal value hadn't dropped by 25%, with the company incurring over $105B in lost value.

One of our biggest challenges is that accountability usually does not come into play until after the fact; after the damage is done and the only recourse shareholders, residents, government or employers have is to fire or incarcerate someone. But what we need is accountability on the front end; in the day to day transactional level of the work that gets done, so we don't have to rely on putting someone's throat in the noose as a form of retribution.

The fact that workers knew the rig had serious problems is a strong indicator that accountability could have been measured and acted on, preventing this and many other serious and not so serious organizational failures.

If you still don't believe that responsibility is the same as accountability, here's another definition that I heard recently,

> Responsibility is what people give you;
> Accountability is what you choose to next!

Accountability is about living up to our commitments. It means you're willing to exceed the expectations of those customers and stakeholders who rely on you and your work. It is about being willing to put in the extra effort to do what you tell your teammates you are going to do and not letting yourself be bullied or intimidated into doing something you know is wrong. It is about doing the right thing, even when you're being pressured to do the wrong thing or encountering obstacles to attaining it.

So, let's stop with the academic exercise of the differences between accountability and responsibility. They essentially mean the same thing, with Responsibility defining the work at hand and Accountability the needs and expectations of our customers and stakeholders as that work is carried out. They are two sides of the same coin.

8. Barriers to Accountability

> *"Your task Is not to seek for love, but merely to seek and find all the barriers within yourself that you have built against it."*
>
> Rumi
> 13th Century Poet

Barriers to accountability are actions (or inactions), cultures or processes that prevent individuals from achieving the needs and expectations of their customers and stakeholders, often necessitating sacrificing one party's needs and expectations for another's.

In my example when I was a Tooling Engineer, I shared one story of how I was unable to be accountable to all my stakeholders. If I was to meet the expectations of one, then I was not able to meet the needs of the other.

In my research leading up to the writing of **Accountable**, I found many articles and books on accountability that insisted it is a willingness to step up and do whatever it takes to be successful. That we simply had to stop making excuses for why we can't achieve and start finding solutions to how we can. Great motivational stuff that speaks directly to the uninspired leader who simply wants to push responsibility on to the workforce. Let them bypass the procedures, adjust the numbers or ignore stakeholder needs and when things inevitably go wrong, they can be blamed.

When I lead teams, I feel it is my responsibility to always be in front of them, identifying and eliminating potential barriers to success before they begin to create turbulence for the team. That's my job…dealing with the policies, procedures, and organizational breakdowns that can prevent my team from achieving success. Then and only then can I expect my team to be accountable and willing to "do whatever it takes".

Throughout my career, I have worked with many organizations across many industries and I have consistently found common barriers to higher levels of accountability. They include:

a) Too Much Chaos

> *"The battlefield is a scene of constant chaos. The winner will be the one who controls that chaos, both his own and the enemies."*
>
> *Napoleon Bonaparte*

Does your workplace resemble a battlefield? Bombs being dropped; people running for cover; snipers taking out anyone willing to stick their head up? In far too many organizations, chaos is the norm, with employees unclear of what work needs to be done, who is responsible for what, where information is being stored. Meetings are filled with never-ending discussions on the same topics again and again. At times, I am surprised we can get anything done at all.

Admittedly, our work is complex and dynamic and even well-orchestrated execution in this environment can seem like chaos but there is a big difference between complex and chaotic. Chaos may be defined as a state of the system where the future development of the system is not predictable and is no longer based on reasonably stable assumptions and goals. Chaos can be on a small isolated scale, resulting in a limited loss of value or it can be all-encompassing, affecting an entire project or organization resulting in dramatic cost and schedule overruns, a loss of functionality or cancellation of entire projects and initiatives or the collapse of an organization.

Can you think of any public or private projects initiatives that were completed on time and on budget? Have you ever been caught up in an organization's confusion loop, where no one seems to know who can take care of your needs and you eventually end up where you started? Missing the mark or getting caught in endless recycle loops is a strong indicator that chaos or the loss of predictability has taken hold.

Chaos is rampant in far too many organizations for four primary reasons;

1) No clarity on the work that needs to get done

I was working on an early stage power project and we needed to get all regulatory and permitting approvals in place prior to sanctioning by our board of directors. In the schedule, we had a single line item. "Construction Permit", so I asked my regulatory lead what was required to get the construction permit. He did not know. "Can you call and ask?" I politely inquired. He came back several days later with a list of 8 documents that would have to be produced to get the Construction Permit, including traffic and landscaping plans, items that could add significant time and effort to pull together if not planned properly.

My experience has shown that people are not naturally adept at clearly defining what has to be done. It takes probing and clarifying questions up front to gain the clarity required to produce a predictable plan.

Most organizations do the same thing over and over again yet have not taken the time to document what they do and how they do it. Work that is poorly defined will tend to spiral out of control much more easily and often, than work that is broken down to the deliverable and task level. Once broken down to this level, it is easy to apply specifications, standards, job aids, tools and best practices to it.

2) No clarity on who can make decisions

Another common cause of chaos is poor or inefficient decision-making. In the top-down management model decision-making authority rarely lies with task authority, which is to say the person doing the work often does not have the decision-making authority to adapt or modify their work based on the circumstances that they encounter. That decision is often moved to another, more senior person in the organization and can take days, weeks, or even months. All too often, that decision is simply avoided leaving people responsible for the work making excuses why no progress is being made.

As the decision moves away from the work front, the sense of urgency is lost; the clarity of related information is diluted and; the situation is often dynamic in nature and changes while a decision is being made.

3) Information Mismanagement

COME ON PEOPLE! We live in the age of information and rarely do I see an organization or project team whose information is nothing short of a disaster. Multiple revisions and versions, some with different names, in random folders with lockdown security, so no one can even access the folders that the information most likely resides in.

4) No Planning

Old school heroes and bullies don't like to plan. They just like to go and figure it out along the way. And I must admit, it's a fun way to work. It's how I do home renovations. I know what I am going to do but I like to let the project evolve along the way rather than have it nailed down too clearly from the beginning.

But in a work setting, without planning, most resources are poorly utilized, and the team can find itself going in directions out of alignment with the organization's strategic vision. Teams get pushed to get started before people understand the needs and expectations and before you know it, they can't meet those needs and expectations because they are going in another direction. Sorry stakeholders.

In this case, the team is off-step and a little confused, and are easy targets for the bullies and heroes to undermine, disrupt or overstep the work that is to be done. Reporting structures often fall apart and progress updates for the project often turns into he said / she said debate which is always won by the person who pounds on the table loudest.

b) Lack of Inspirational Leadership

> "Our chief want is someone who will inspire us to be what we know we could be."
>
> \- Ralph Waldo Emerson

In the ccOS, leaders kick people in the ass with increasing intensity and frequency to get things done. That really translates into bullying, intimidation, threats and whatever subversive means they can use. In the tdOS, leaders use prescriptive processes and a combination of carrot rewards and stick punishments to get people engaged and working at a higher level. In the hOS, leaders inspire people to be dedicated to the success of the organization, accountable to meet obligations and supportive of their team members to drive project and organizational success.

The HOW Report shows that Inspired workers are 27% more predictive of performance than their engaged counterparts and offers four qualities that Inspirational Leaders require;

Scaling Values

Instilling a deep commitment to values and to a set of standards to which people at all levels of the organization hold themselves accountable.

Pursuing Significance

Enlisting all employees in a commitment to a shared purpose-inspired mission that speaks to them as individuals, ignites their passion and unifies them in a meaningful endeavor.

Heightening Consciousness

Building healthy, sustainable interdependency and connectedness among employees, partners, and stakeholders, extending to its customers and society at large.

Fostering Freedom

Creating space by carefully promoting freedom from traditional constraints like hierarchy, and filling that space with carefully nurtured freedom to express oneself, experiment and exercise leadership

With only 8% of organizations using an Inspirational Leadership model, most of today's management and executive leaders only know how to use coercion or motivation to get people to act and to join. They lack the competencies required to create a context for long-term thinking, or the team development skills to create high-performance work environments, or the patience, empathy or ego to let others be the best they can be.

One last important point from the HOW report...the challenge of Lack of Inspirational Leadership gets significantly worse as organizational size grows and as you move down the organizational ladder. C-Suites are five times as likely to have an empowered work environment than their operational and front-line counterparts.

c) Lack of understanding

> *"Furious activity is no substitute for understanding."*
>
> *- H.H Williams*
> *Philosophy Instructor and Bishop of Carlisle*

To be accountable, people must have a strong understanding of WHY they are doing what they are doing. Without such contextual knowledge, we all too often end up fixing something that didn't need to be fixed or miss something that did. We get caught up jumping into the work without having a clear understanding of why we are doing the work. We ask, "How do I accomplish this?", and "What do I do now or next?" and although those questions are good to ask, they often take center stage and overshadow the Why.

Thinking from the inside out, understanding the Why before focusing on the How and the What ensures that actions are in alignment with needs and expectations.

I was recently talking to a friend who works in a metal fabrication and machine repair business about an issue they had recently. A customer had an emergency repair of a bearing surface that needed to be completed ASAP. He called the shop and gave a detailed explanation of the problem while rushing the broken part to their shop.

The Order Desk, who took the call, contacted the Shop Foreman and told him a part was coming in for repair, with little of the detail transferred by the customer. Upon receipt, no time was wasted discussing the issue and the part was set up in a fixture on the floor and damage was analyzed and the repair began by the Welder in minutes. Once complete, the part had to be properly heat treated before being shipped back to the customer.

When the customer got the part, they quickly realized that the repair had only addressed one of the damaged surfaces, so had to be returned to the shop for another repair. The customer ended up being down for two extra days resulting in additional lost revenue.

This may not seem like a significant issue, but insignificant issues like this happen every day in organizations, creating rework and losses, while igniting chaos, as shop planning is quickly overridden by heroic interventions.

The accountability for this failure lies with every person along the work chain:

a) Customer

The customer only provided a verbal description of a bearing surface that needed to be repaired. They provided no drawings, pictures or sketches to clarify what work needed to be done. They assumed the shop would understand and they did not inspire the Order Desk clerk to fully understand the problem.

b) Order Desk

The Order Desk did not really understand the problem but made notes of the What...the work that needed to be done. At no time did they ask for pictures or marked up drawings that would help them to truly understand the problem and avoid an upset customer.

c) Shop Foreman

The same goes for the Shop Foreman. He merely took the What at face value and began to plan the How; how the repair would be done, without understanding the part being repaired, what its application was and why it had failed?

d) Welder

The same goes for the Welder.

Now the customer calls the Order Desk and yells at the young clerk working there. The Order Desk calls their boss and reports the unhappy client. The boss tears a strip off the Shop Foreman for not doing the entire repair the first time and the Shop Foreman berates the Welder and questions his competency, to which the Welder replies, "You never told me to repair the other surface. I didn't know".

And that is where it ends...for another day.

d) Lack of Initiative

> *"Have the backbone to take the initiative and lead the way. Just make sure you have a box to pack your stuff when they fire your ass for not asking for permission!"*
>
> \- Unknown

We've all read those leadership books that tell us that leadership can happen at any level. That we don't have to be at the top of the org chart or have a title to be a leader. And sure enough, many of the greatest leadership stories are about those people who didn't let a lack of authority or position affect their determination to lead change.

But in command and control organizations, leadership is equated with insubordination. It's doing things that you have been told not to do or have not been given authority to do and that is grounds for reprimand or dismissal. These organizations wonder why their staff resembles the cast of the Walking Dead but then squash, suppress or punish initiative every chance they get.

I once worked with an engineer who shared a story that will always stick with me. We were a bright and ambitious group and we were always coming up with ideas on how to improve the business. He liked to describe the idea as a ball. He would excitedly go to our boss with this ball in his hand and say, "Look at the great idea I have. It will save the company money and drive higher levels of customer satisfaction!"

The boss would look at the ball, open the top drawer of his desk, which was filled with other colorful balls, throw it in, close the drawer and say, "Get back to work". The boss thought we were giving him the ball, but we were just asking for permission to pursue it further. Now the ball was in the boss' hand and if my colleague were to pursue it, it would be in direct conflict with the boss as he now controlled the ball.

More recently, I had an idea for a project that would benefit the community in which I was working. I was a newcomer and was curious about how to initiate such a project, so I asked my manager how to approach the local committee that would likely oversee such a project (my manager happened to sit on that committee).

"Do you have any idea how much work that would create for me?" She ranted at me in response. "If I did that then they would expect me to be responsible for this, that and the other…"

I was a little confused. I had not asked my manager to do anything. I was just trying to figure out how the process worked so that I could then take a leadership role for my cause. Now I would be going behind her back if I tried to implement it. I had to drop the idea.

Heroes struggle with ideas and initiatives that are not their own. They simply respond by saying "I don't have the time to deal with this." Yet workers aren't looking for managers to solve the problem or implement their idea, they are simply looking for approval or the opening of a door to the decision makers who can approve it so that they can become leaders.

e) Lack of Authority

> *"The disappearance of a sense of responsibility is the most far-reaching consequence of submission to authority."*
>
> \- Stanley Milgram
>
> Social Psychologist, known for his studies on obedience

People typically have not been granted the requisite level of authority they need to drive success in their responsibilities. That authority works in three ways:

1. Decision-making

If our managers don't give us the authority to make decisions…if they manage not just what we do but make the decisions on our behalf, we can't be accountable to our stakeholders.

If decision-making is stripped away from the work that we do, we become responsible for work that we may not agree with and have no control over. Worse yet, we become responsible for the implementation of our manager's directives which all too often don't take stakeholder needs into consideration.

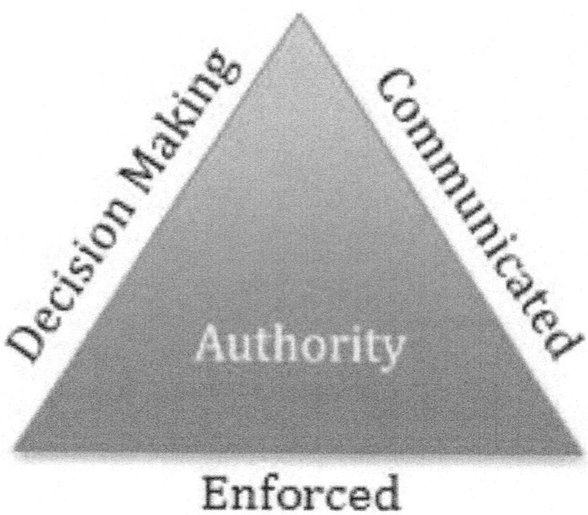

Figure 11: Authority Triangle

2. Communication

Have you ever been given responsibility for a task, but your manager refuses to tell anyone? I have, far too often. By not publicly granting authority, others, especially those in positions higher than our own, tend to look at us with suspicion, especially when we need them to do something to achieve our objective.

To empower people with the right level of authority, it is critical to publicly state who is responsible for what. I work with teams to develop a responsibility matrix to better communicate and manage the tasks and expectations across the organization, then use it to manage misalignment and conflict across the team.

3. Enforcement

The third side of the authority triangle is ensuring people respect individual responsibilities and treat them as an important customer when providing services. If other team members can ignore the needs and expectations of the responsible person, or worse yet, simply override them, organizational leadership must be willing to intervene and hold that person accountable to their commitments. I like to call this turf management.

When you rely on other people to do work that supports and provides inputs to your own, you are the customer; you are the one who sets expectations. And if you don't have the proper authority, those who are supposed to serve you, ignore your needs and now you can't live up to your accountabilities.

Often those individuals who are accountable to us are above us on the organizational chart or even our customers and this is where accountability completely falls apart in the command and control work environment. Anyone higher on the organization chart or working for the customer too often feel that they can't be told what to do by someone "below them"!

I was doing a project for a large computer manufacturer which included the production of some plastic computer parts and sub-assemblies. Our client was responsible for delivering one of the parts required in the subassembly and we weren't getting any updates from them on their status. But the person managing the project (who was my client) would simply get angry with me and tell me to mind my own business. "Remember who the client is!" she liked to sneer.

Part of our contract was to provide cosmetic parts in time for a marketing photo shoot that had a hard date for completion or the entire project could be severely impacted. If we missed the date, there would be financial penalties.

During our initial trials with our client, she began to override my decision-making authority and insist that pressure levels were too high, and the tooling must be reworked before we could proceed. I knew if we did not produce usable samples that day, our schedule-driven project would be late, and I would be held accountable.

When the client left the shop floor, I discussed the issue with my Mold Technician to analyze risks of damage to the tooling if something failed from an overpressure situation (pressure in injection molding can exceed 30,000psi). If we were to proceed without her blessing and something went wrong, I would be out of a job.

We both agreed the risks were minimal, so we started the machine back up and began increasing the pressure until we were making complete parts that met the identified needs and expectations as defined in the original contract; with no damage to the tooling.

Shortly thereafter, the customer reappeared and was in dismay when she realized that we had proceeded to make parts despite her directive not to. She was pissed and did everything she could to get me fired. I knew I was taking a risk by "doing whatever it takes" to meet my commitments and I knew I was taking a risk by not doing it. Damned if I do, damned if I don't. That's the situation too many workers are put in organizations that lack clarity and accountability.

In ccOS and tdOS, the customer is always right. In hOS, the customer is accountable, just like everyone else. My company took the client's side and began a process of undermining, marginalizing and bullying me until I handed in my resignation two months later.

f) Lack of Process

> *"Inconsistency is the only thing at which men are consistent."*
>
> *Horace Smith*
> *Co-founder of Smith and Wesson*

Most work gets done using processes and procedures, but in many ccOS organizations, they consist of undocumented tribal knowledge that is difficult to measure, monitor or hold people accountable to.

For the newcomer, it seems a lot like a mystery, almost impossible to understand. To the bully, it's an opportunity to move the goalposts to ensure they succeed and you fail. While to the hero, procedures are something to be bypassed to get to the end goal faster, with little regard for the negative impacts their actions have on others.

It is also important to understand that although you may see opportunity in upgrading your processes, the current informal process can be an important time-saving starting point. For one, they work, as cumbersome, clunky and unscalable as they may be. And two, you already have buy-in from the current team because it's how they do it.

I was working with one organization asking frontline supervisors how their informal processes worked and what could be changed to make their lives better. Every time, I found enthusiastic leaders who wanted to make the processes better and were more than willing to do what it took to support such a change. But all too often they would say things like,

"You know, no one has ever asked me that before. Usually, people come in here with a solution and they haven't asked one person what they need or what their ideas are for fixing the system".

Collaboratively redesigning your organizational processes is a critical step in developing buy-in and commitment to the new processes and driving higher levels of accountability.

g) Too Much Process

> *"When people's jobs depend on meeting metrics and maintaining the status quo, can you fault them for their reluctance to expend any energy toward creation and invention?."*
>
> *Lisa Bodell*
> *Author, futurist, and CEO of futurethink*

In tdOS systems, processes are usually exceptionally prescriptive, limiting a person's ability to add value, solve problems and drive customer satisfaction. A recent study[8] by The Boston Consulting Group found that "over the past fifteen years, the amount of procedures, vertical layers, interface structures, coordination bodies, and decision approvals needed…has increased by anywhere from 50 percent to 350 percent." What's more, many "managers spend 40 percent of their time writing reports and 30 percent to 60 percent of it in coordination meetings."

I recently called the Canada Revenue Agency for an audit they were doing for my Child Tax Benefit following the separation from my wife. They wanted to get two witnesses who could verify when I had moved out of our shared dwelling.

I told the first person that no one other than my ex-wife and I would know those dates, so he told me he was sorry but that was what was required and if I could not comply, the government would decide without my input. He inferred that perhaps I could tell the witnesses what the dates were despite a stern warning that any false or misleading statements were a federal offense.

I called them back, telling a second customer service person that I could not identify any people who could confirm the dates, other than my ex-wife and I, and we had never been asked. It pissed me off that the government had never even asked me for this information in the first place and were now auditing it. I was told that "that is how the process works and thousands of these audits are sent out every year".

I told her that they needed to fix their process because it was expensive, an infringement on my personal rights and an intrusion in my life during a very difficult time.

She pointed out that our conversation was going in circles

I suggested that she be replaced by a form!

She hung up on me.

They were unable and unwilling to understand or meet my needs and expectations. In the top-down management model, stakeholders rarely have a say. They simply must follow the procedures that were set up with little consideration for their needs and do what you are told. Even when you are the customer!

I was also recently reading about the Canadian Transportation Agency's review of the Air Transat story about two planeloads of people that sat on a sweltering tarmac last summer for up to six hours with no food, or fresh air and little water. It wasn't until someone finally dialed 911 that the situation was resolved, and passengers could deplane.

The Canadian Transport Agency took Air Transit to task, saying that AT policies did not adequately consider passengers needs and rights when planes are diverted, staff were not properly trained to deal with a plane diversions and de-planing and they failed to live up to their own "Terms and Conditions of Carriage" related to passenger disembarkment and to the distribution of drinks and snacks.

It also stated that AT was not relieved of its obligations simply because events beyond its control required diversion of the flights or because the actions of other parties contributed to the length of the delays. The company failed to properly meet the needs of the customers who were in their care, custody, and control.

But where were the compassionate front-line workers who were witnessing and were part of the discomfort? Why did they not have more empathy for the passengers and intervene; open the door and order a few pizzas? The pilot had final say on deplaning and resisted doing so for some reason other than the needs of the passengers. But at what point does the pilot's responsibility for control of the aircraft (operation and safety) get overridden by the attendants' responsibility for the care and custody of the passengers. Or are the attendants always subservient to the pilots and have no true authority?

Rigid processes which ignore extenuating circumstances or any real understanding of the bigger purpose of our work undermine our powerful capability of adapting to the needs and expectations of our customers and stakeholders, and are best assigned to computers and robots, not people.

h) Lack of Competency

> *"Your driver is on the steer, driving you and you can feel free to doze in the car; this is trust built on competence. Competence is to ensure that your actions put people's hearts at ease when things are in your hands."*
>
> — *Israelmore Ayivor*
> Inspirational writer and entrepreneur

People are often thrown into situations without the experience or competency required to be successful. When this happens, it's the manager's responsibility to either provide the appropriate support for that person, which builds their personal and your organizational capacity or they can decide to reassign the task to someone who is competent in that area. The problem is, many people don't trust their organizations enough to admit to a lack of competency and won't ask for help.

I recently read a story about two workers who were killed at Nexen's Long Lake facility in northern Alberta. They were tasked with a repair to a piece of equipment on which they had no experience or demonstrated competency in fixing. That lack of competency cost them their lives. There were other extenuating circumstances beyond simple competency, there always are in chaotic and toxic work environments, but if the two men had the training and experience they needed they likely would not have made the mistakes that eventually lead to their death.

It is not to say people can't take on tasks that they have never done. When I was first assigned the task of developing a team-building plan for a multibillion-dollar industrial project, I embraced it, although I had never done it before. The internet gave me unlimited access to information on the topic and I could pull together a solid plan, but I really lacked the experience in its implementation, thus, my efforts had limited impact. If I was repairing a high-pressure vessel like the guys at Nexen, I too would have been killed.

If you look at any organizational loss of value, whether it's a workplace injury, a project going over budget or having an exceptionally high turnover rate, a lack of competency is a major contributor to that loss. We demand more and more of our workforce in terms of competency while our school systems fail to provide the skills necessary to contribute in a bigger way. Meanwhile, corporations are reluctant to invest in competency training with an increasingly transient workforce.

In a study I did many years ago, I analyzed the competency levels of an organization's Service Technicians. This role was critical to the overall success of the organization due to their direct impact on customer satisfaction scores and future sales.

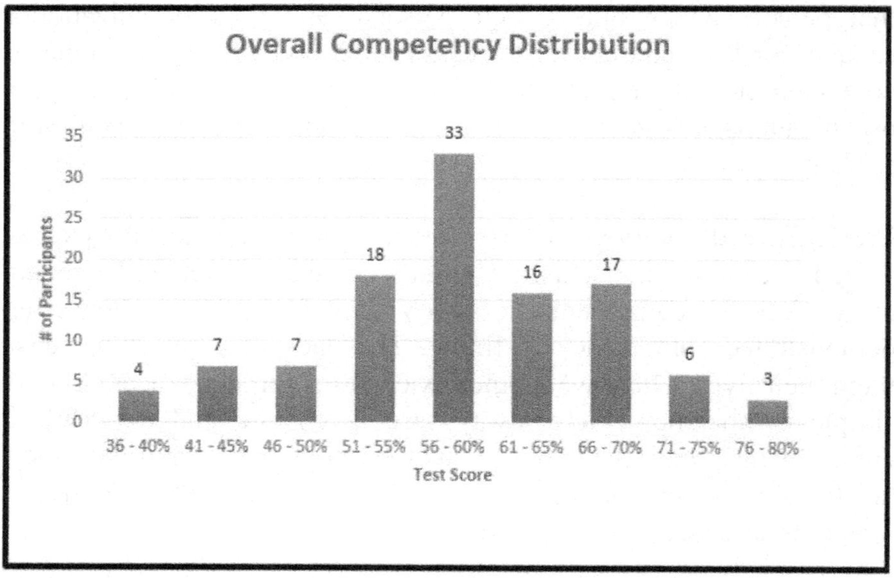

Figure 12: Knowledge Distribution for Service Technicians

What I found was that the average Service Technician had 58% of the knowledge they required to be successful and no one had 100%. The highest scores were just under 80% and those were found to be the technicians that were known for driving higher levels of customer service. There was a direct correlation between competency and customer service.

From that work, I hypothesized that most knowledge workers did not have the knowledge or competency they required to always be successful and the more complex the job, the worse the situation likely was.

Often, worker's refuse to admit to their incompetencies for fear of being micromanaged or removed from the job altogether. I once conceded to my command and control manager that I felt my knowledge of part design was limiting my success working on a consumer product launch. I was not actually designing the parts, but I felt it would help me to better understand what could and could not be done from a manufacturing perspective. A week later, I was taken off the job.

I reached out to him and admitted my weakness not because I didn't think I could do the job, rather I needed some support or training to better enable me to do the job. I learned then and there to never admit weakness in a command and control work environment.

If people aren't competent; if they lack the underlying skill and knowledge, or if they have never had the experience to develop the competency, they will not and should not assume responsibility for the work without proper support and oversight, especially if the work is important and has significant exposure if things go wrong, such as the death of the workers I mentioned earlier. It is the manager's job to identify where those gaps are and lean in to provide higher levels of support and oversight if we expect that inexperienced person to be successful.

i) Lack of Time

> *"Many time pressures, along with conflicts between work and family, can be resolved simply by letting people schedule their time themselves and be rewarded for the results they produce, instead of for being visible."*
>
> - Lotte Baylin
> MIT Professor
> from "The Dance of Change"

Top-down organizations and micromanagers tend to not only manage our decisions but also our time. A recent survey showed that 68% of respondents agreed that their manager's priorities change frequently creating confusion and undermining success around the key results they were trying to achieve. By empowering people to manage their own time, we would get everything done and more. But those top-down managers are too busy giving direction; often counter to the direction they had given only earlier that same day.

It's not only about how we organize and prioritize our time, it's what we spend our time doing that is a significant challenge. I watched a documentary recently that claimed that 60% of the paperwork performed in many organizations has nothing to do with the customer, and 40% of the work adds no value at all. It's no wonder we don't have any time!

This excess paperwork is a strong sign of poor accountability. We don't get more accountable by reporting to others who are trying to make our decisions and manage our time. We get more accountable by reporting progress, issues, and concerns to our customers and stakeholders.

I recently had a friend tell me about a boss who had started asking for daily work summaries from his team because he had to watch things more closely. Who am I to say that a daily report doesn't add value, but these individuals then refuse to acknowledge the tremendous level of effort required to meet these superfluous demands. We apply willful blindness while we pour yet more work on an overextended and increasingly unproductive workforce.

When we impose impossible requirements on our team members, we put them in the unenviable position of not meeting the needs and expectations of stakeholders; of having to break the rules to do so. How can we be accountable for something we don't have time to do? People can only take on so much workload and put in so many hours before they either bend or break.

Bending means they adapt by "prioritizing"; they stop doing certain things to create time, which then passes the problem on to someone else in the value chain, compounding the problem. One of the first things people cut out to save time is getting clarity on customer and stakeholder needs and expectations; in other words, we save time but not truly understanding what it is we're doing.

In the book "Fixit; Getting Accountability Right[9]", the authors found that 77% of workers and 62% of leaders don't take the time to obtain the perspective of others. Next is a lack of proper planning which often results in missteps and a loss of organizational value by not thinking an issue through properly before acting. A third area is bypassing quality procedures which then result in rework or product failure.

Breaking means your employees snap, resulting in aggression, stress leave, resignation or a heart attack. In fact, a study[10] in 2009 by Sweden Psychologist Anna Nyberg, found that your risk of heart attack increases by 40% when you work for a mean-spirited micromanager.

Top-down cultures tend to underestimate the time and energy necessary to do the job right because they don't understand how chaotic and bureaucratic their workplaces have become. The result is frustration, incivility, and mediocrity. Our limited resources end up spending their time chasing their tails fighting the resultant fires rather than doing the job right in the first place.

j) Lack of Transparency

> *"There is not a crime, there is not a dodge, there is not a trick, there is not a swindle, there is not a vice which does not live by secrecy."*
>
> — Joseph Pulitzer
> American Newspaper Publisher

Without transparency, open access to information and a willingness to be honest, you cannot have accountability. Privacy is often a veil to hide the negative impacts an organizational initiative is going to have. Command and control managers will insist that hiding bad news is a valid way to drive success, avoiding conflict with stakeholders.

I have had organizational leaders say, "If we consulted everybody on everything, we wouldn't get anything done." And in command and control, he's right. Their mindset is to get things done before people become aware of the negative impacts they are really having.

Transparency is a difficult challenge to overcome as it is intertwined with liability, for things we did and didn't do, and competency, allowing our work to be scrutinized by our stakeholders. Command and control leaders tend to exaggerate good information while hiding bad, creating a shroud of secrecy around the knowledge they hold.

Inspirational leaders communicate updates, decisions, issues facing the organization, challenges in the marketplace, and successes across the organization. They know that for people to contribute at a higher level they must understand the challenges, successes, and opportunities that will determine future organizational success.

They provide the vision of what is coming and what is needed, then enlist the power and experience of the entire organization to identify creative solutions to their challenges. They raise the brain power by a factor of 10 to drive solutions that not only meet their needs, but that creates win-win successes that meet many more stakeholders needs.

Being transparent with stakeholders ensures that they have been given an opportunity to state their concerns, objections, expectations, and ideas. Avoiding those conversations will only lead to conflict, churn, chaos and the associated organizational losses.

k) Lack of Confidence

> "When you have confidence, you can have a lot of fun. And when you have fun, you can do amazing things."
>
> Joe Namath
> NFL Hall of Fame Quarterback

After years of having been told what to do, many people simply don't have the confidence required to take a leadership role regarding their responsibilities. They just want their micro-manager to tell them what to do and they blindly do it. Without such direct intervention, many of our workers will get mired down in the decision-making process.

I had an engineering lead working for me on a project who struggled with making decisions. He had a bully for a boss and had a pretty non-confrontational personality. His boss wanted to make all the decisions but as the project manager, I did not allow that. I wanted my people to make their own decisions and take ownership of those decisions.

On one specific issue, we had three options for a solution. I asked the lead which option he was going to choose and he told me. Then I asked him why and he responded, "Because my boss told me to do it that way." That was the wrong answer for me and it was not the answer I wanted to tell the client when they would inevitably ask.

When our team members just do what they are told, they lose their sense of ownership and accountability and they begin to willfully ignore negative impacts of their decisions because to see them and raise them would be to question their bully micromanager of a boss and that scares the hell out of them.

In the example above, my lead knew there were advantages to one of the other designs, but he refused to create an issue over it and he willingly increased the cost of that transaction.

What if the oversight was catastrophic? The boss might say "That person should have known better".

While the employee will respond, "I was just doing what I was told".

Making good decisions is not an easy thing. It is difficult to always create win-win solutions that please all your stakeholders and sometimes our decisions will result in conflict and confrontation. That is the hard part about accountability. But it is critical that we help people to make their own decisions related to their responsibilities.

That does not mean the manager can stand back and watch a disaster unfold, rather, it is their responsibility to coach and ask questions regarding their employees' decisions to make sure they have considered all the stakeholder needs and have made the best decision in relation to the interest of the project, initiative or organization.

Using terms like, "How does that help us achieve our vision of success?" or "How does that meet the needs of the stakeholders?" will help the person to frame their decision in the proper context and be able to adjust it to better suit the need or justify the decision that they made.

If the person still can't make their own decision and simply wants to be told what to do, as their manager you have the responsibility to take that responsibility away from that person as they do not have the confidence, or perhaps competency, to handle the decision-making authority associated with it.

l) Heroism

> *"The hero syndrome is a phenomenon affecting people who seek heroism or recognition, usually by creating a desperate situation which they can resolve."*
>
> *From Wikipedia, the free encyclopedia*

Many of our organizations, whether they be corporations, project teams or volunteer committees, are run by a "hero culture", a small group of hard-working, highly talented "heroes" who get things done with little assistance, on sheer strength, will and knowledge.

These heroes typically put in long hours (and they are more than happy to tell you how many) to get the job done and fundamentally believe others don't have the knowledge, skill, experience, or drive needed. Those people need to simply get out of the way, so they can do great things.

Heroes are instrumental in helping organizations forge new trails; to move into uncharted territory where there are no existing maps, no processes or job instructions. They figure out the business on the fly. The notion of a hero culture is not limited to start-ups or entrepreneurial ventures, they can be found in any organization regardless of size or maturity.

All this heroism comes at a price. These organizations tend to be very inefficient and have wildly varying levels of success. Heroes thrive in a state of chaos, so they tend to undermine any initiative designed to bring clarity and order to a situation. And although the hero is available to save the day, rarely do they stick around to determine the underlying cause and develop a long-term solution to eliminate the recurring problem.

Everything is stored in the hero's head as tribal knowledge. They lack the agility to respond to rapidly changing conditions or complexity such as dealing with a multitude of stakeholders or increasingly stringent regulatory requirements. Sadly, we also can't leverage the knowledge, skill, and experience of the hero to grow the business, we can only hire more heroes. But heroes typically don't like sharing the limelight with other heroes.

To the non-heroic newcomer, these organizations seem incredibly chaotic. They find it impossible to figure out how things get done and are often marginalized to the sidelines watching rather than contributing. Heroes burst onto the scene, guns blazing while everyone else runs for cover.

At the end of the carnage, the dutiful, non-hero staff are left with the job of cleaning up the messes created by the heroes…they aren't good at doing paperwork, managing details, following up with stakeholders or taking responsibility when things go wrong.

Organizations can't afford to have most of their staff on the sidelines, running for cover. They need them to drive organizational efficiency, consistency, and continuous improvement. That can't happen until the organization commits to transforming from a hero-based culture to one of collaboration and accountability.

m) Micromanagement

> *"It doesn't make sense to hire smart people and then tell them what to do. We hire smart people, so they can tell us what to do!"*
>
> *- Steve Jobs*
> *Founder, Apple Inc.*

I recently read an article[12] written by iconic business leader Jack Welch praising the power of micromanagement. To be fair, he recognizes the difference between "jerk bosses" who think that they should make the decisions associated with responsibilities and perfectly good bosses who do the same kind of thing because they recognize the individual is not yet ready to take on full responsibility. The latter provide supports where required and provide leadership, so the individual can gain confidence and strength in their responsibilities.

Successful managers know how to lean into individuals and situations that require additional support. They know when to get involved and when to let people take ownership. When to coach, when to mentor, when to act as a senior advisor and when to step in and take the responsibility away.

And they know when to lean back recognizing increased levels of competence, confidence and efficiency are beginning to take root, so they no longer need to take control of the work. Successful managers know whether the type of support is expertise, authoritative, experiential or monitoring and they can switch between these options seamlessly as the protégé increases in ability.

Micromanagement is often the simple act of withholding decision-making authority out of fear that others will fail. Micromanagers often have insatiable fears that someone is going to make a bad decision and it's going to affect their reputation or position in the organization, so they quickly intervene and take over. Not to say it might not be the right thing to do at times, but micromanagers assume they are responsible for everything, all the time.

Managers who want to drive higher levels of accountability try to understand why that person is failing and offer support or eliminate barriers to success before using their position, power, and authority to take over someone's decision-making authority or responsibility. And even if they do, they make a case for why it's important for them to take over. This approach and mindset forms a cornerstone for continuously growing organizational capacity.

Micromanagers also ignore complexities to make faster, less accurate decisions that meet few stakeholders' needs. When I teach project management courses, I like to tell my students that in the old days, you just had to make your boss and your boss' boss happy. Now you must keep a wide array of internal and external stakeholders happy. That reflects the increasing complexity of our work. A complexity that micromanagement and the top-down management models struggle with.

Micromanagers tend to think their job is to just show up and make decisions and solve every problem. During meetings, they bark orders rather than listening to the team about the help that they need. They typically want to be involved in every meeting, decision and often communication. Thus, they become a massive bottleneck in the organization. As the backlog of decisions builds and the challenges associated with historical bad decisions becomes insurmountable, everything slows to a crawl.

Sometimes micromanagement is just a sense of entitlement. Decision-making authority is something that comes with tenure and position, not with individual responsibility. And that sense of entitlement can be a powerful resisting force to a more collaborative environment. If those now in power feel they are giving away the one thing they worked so hard for, decision-making authority, then they will fight any initiative to drive decision-making back to the level where the work is getting done.

When a decision is being made by someone removed from the workface, they must be willing to take on the entire responsibility of the task, deliverable or decisions. That includes understanding the stakeholders, meeting their needs and doing their paperwork! Too many micromanagers feel they are above paperwork, process and accountability to the team and outside stakeholders. That creates chaos, contempt and a big mess to clean up when the micromanager thinks the job is done.

Jack Welch concedes that micromanaging only stinks when bosses do it because they have nothing better to do, or they're constitutionally unable to trust people.

Too often, I have seen managers working one or two levels below where they should be, making decisions related to tasks being performed by the people below them. As a result, not only are their responsibilities not getting done, but the people who are supposed to be doing the work are now standing back waiting to be told what to do next.

In Welch's conclusion, he states, "When your level of micromanaging grows out of strong, vibrant engagement with your people, have no fear. When you get involved, your team will know you're in it for them. And when you step back, they'll be in it for you too." Great words of wisdom indeed, but not in alignment with the simplistic and marginalizing behavior of what I call micromanagement and see far too often.

9. Guiding Values of Accountability

> *"Your beliefs become your thoughts, your thoughts become your words, your words become your actions, your actions become your habits, your habits become your values, your values become your destiny."*
>
> *– Mahatma Gandhi*
>
> Preeminent leader of India's independence movement

Values are traits or qualities that represent an individual's highest priorities and deepest beliefs. They define what we believe to be appropriate actions and reflect a person's sense of right or wrong. Increasingly, organizations are adopting values and value statements to help drive a culture that is more in alignment with the vision of the organization's leadership.

Sadly, too many organization's struggle with living up to those values…possibly because they don't have a way of monitoring success in their implementation. Can you measure trust or respect? It's pretty tough. But values are critical to helping the team define "how" they are going to achieve a higher level of accountability.

To create impact from values, an organization needs to;

- Demonstrate and model values in everything they do.
- Use values to set priorities, guide decisions and actions.
- Recognize and reward application of values
- Integrate values into team goals
- Hire and promote individuals whose outlook and actions exemplify the team's values.

Corporate culture has little to do with espoused values and everything to do with actual values and experiences people bring to the job. If you want your organization to embrace an accountable approach, my experience has shown that you must be willing to embrace the following values and reward those that demonstrate them in their actions and decisions.

a) Trust

> *"There is one thing that is common to every individual, relationship, team, family, organization, nation, economy and civilization throughout the world – one thing which if removed will destroy the most powerful government, the most successful business, the most thriving economy, the most influential leadership, the greatest friendship, the strongest character, the deepest love.*
>
> *On the other hand, if developed and leveraged, that one thing has the potential to create unparalleled success and prosperity in every dimension of life. Yet it is the least understood, most neglected and most underestimated possibility of our time. That one thing is trust."*
>
> *Stephen M.R, Covey*
> *Author, The Speed of Trust*

Possibly the most important and most difficult enabler of accountability is a sense of trust; trust that your employees will make decisions that are in the best interest of the company; trust that the organization will support you and have your back; trust that people can say what is on their mind; and trust you won't be reprimanded for taking a stand on what is important.

I once worked for a company whose leadership told me I trusted my team too much! I am a highly collaborative person who tries to demonstrate openness and honesty and I want my team to have confidence in my intentions and in my ability. My leadership team seemed to believe that people were lazy liars who could not be trusted and whom I could only get higher levels of productivity and success from, by kicking them in the ass; to trust your employees was to be taken for a fool. I couldn't disagree with them more.

If you can build a trusting team, you will achieve great things and you will have a lot of fun doing it, despite the pressures, challenges, and obstacles that you and your team face. With strong trust, we build strong awareness of each other, agility, resilience and an increased likelihood of developing innovative solutions to your problems.

Conversely, top-down, hero cultures tend to be built on deception, where people withhold information, hide issues and are unclear in defining their needs and expectations. This lack of clarity results in a dramatic decline in team trust and a loss of performance.

Building trust is a slow, continuous process. By trusting others, they begin to trust us. But that trust can be eroded instantaneously when we allow the hero culture to intervene, especially in times of crisis. We must trust the process, trust each other's commitment to the process and to each other, and trust that everyone will do what is best for the organization and its objectives. That's not blind trust. That's trust built on discussion and dialogue to create a common understanding and objective. Trust is not free, and it certainly isn't easy. A leader must be willing to do the hard work required to build a high trust culture.

Throughout my career, people opened up to me because I was able to create an environment of trust, they told me their concerns and I worked hard to help them overcome their challenges, so they were able to meet their commitments. And because people trusted me, they did more, they implemented their ideas and they were willing to change.

In the book, "Trust Works! Four Keys to Building Lasting Relationships"[9], Ken Blanchard and fellow authors found that trust was the key element of successful Organizational Change Management (OCM) initiatives and they identify four attributes to developing trust.

1) Able

Team members earn trust by solving problems, getting results, and using their skills to help others achieve their goals.

2) Believable

Team members earn trust by being honest and sincere, showing respect for others, keeping confidences, not talking behind people's backs, and admitting their own mistakes. In other words, they act with integrity.

3) Connected

Team members earn trust by showing interest in others, asking for input, listening, showing empathy, praising others' efforts, and sharing about themselves.

4) Dependable

Team members earn trust by being organized, timely, accountable, and responsive to requests; they do what they say they'll do and consistently follow up.

b) Respect

> *There is a great deal of talk about loyalty from the bottom to the top. Loyalty from the top-down is even more necessary and much less prevalent. One of the most frequently noted characteristics of great men who have remained great is loyalty to their subordinates.*
>
> *- General George S Patton*
> *United States Army*

In top-down environments, the expectation is often that loyalty and respect need only flow up through the organizational hierarchy. In an accountable environment, it flows in all directions. Disrespect happens in a myriad of ways and all must be challenged if you want to drive higher levels of accountability. It can include;

- Not respecting individual decision-making authority
- Speaking ill of others
- Ignoring needs, expectations, concerns, and requests
- Belittling
- Undermining
- Invalidating

Without a culture of mutual loyalty and respect, the potential of your team will never be realized.

I recently had a manager begin to question me regarding one of my responsibilities that had not been a priority, but for some reason, they began getting frustrated with me because no action was being taken. To them, this seemed like an affront to their authority, but I was simply dealing with issues that were much more critical to the organization and its stakeholders.

They began treating me like I was incompetent and did not understand how to do my job. They dictated, not what they needed and what their expectations were, but how I was to do my job. I was yelled at for not doing what I was told. It all turned ugly so fast. I questioned whether I should be terminating my contract. They questioned whether they should do the same. I felt a complete lack of respect. They did too.

This is typical of how a mutual lack of respect for individual responsibilities leads to conflict, resignation (spiritually and contractually) and a completely unnecessary crisis. This example not only speaks to the importance of respect but of clarity of who was responsible for what. My manager felt that they were responsible to get the work done; I felt that I was. It's tough to respect individual responsibilities when you don't agree who IS responsible.

Mutual respect means respecting the autonomy associated with each team member's responsibilities. I once met a young female engineer from Venezuela. She struck me as a thoughtful, perhaps slightly quiet person who struggled at work because her more aggressive male counterparts took her quiet thoughtful approach as meaning that she "didn't have the stuff" to get the job done and simply started giving direction and making decisions on her part. That is not respect, that's bullying.

Another friend works with a co-facilitator, who has been with the organization longer and considers themselves to be the senior facilitator and thus tends to take charge and give orders rather than be a co-facilitator. Because of that approach, my friend feels that their personality and creativity are not allowed to shine. They feel stifled and frustrated because they have a lot more to contribute to the organizational and individual success but can't.

Perhaps more common in the workplace is the disrespect associated with rumor and talking behind each other's backs. If I talk about coworkers' shoddy workmanship, about a manager's crude remarks at a meeting, or a suggestion that someone was promoted for nefarious reasons, it's all disrespect.

Respect is being willing to stand up for the team's individual and collective values and being willing to provide your team with the positive feedback they need to be better every day. The ability to give and receive feedback and coaching is a critical part of successful teams and demonstrates respect and trust daily.

c) Collaboration

> *"Collaboration isn't about giving up our individuality; it's about realizing our greater potential."*
>
> *— Joseph Rain*
> *Author & Entrepreneur*

One of the most significant changes in the 21st century is our ability to use technology to network, connect, share information and ideas and to create holistic solutions that meet the needs of the many. This unprecedented social connectivity can allow us to reinvent our institutions and organizations if we embrace and allow it to permeate our guiding vision.

Connectivity can be the lever to finally embrace collaboration and begin to create simple solutions to complex issues. We need to build tools to discuss what we are doing and what we are learning. We need to connect those who have with those who need; we need to create forums for discussion, debate, and dialogue, both one-on-one and en masse; and we need to reward those people who embrace a more collaborative approach.

We don't need one size fits all solutions! We need unique solutions for every stakeholder group and individual. And we can only achieve that level of complexity by tapping into the wealth of skill, knowledge, and experience that exists within our teams. Traditional power structures of hierarchy and rank tend to undermine a leader's ability to build collaborative cultures.

As leadership guru John Maxwell says, "If you want to achieve your full potential, you have to do it with others."

d) Openness and Transparency

> *"The best weapon of a dictatorship is secrecy, but the best weapon of a democracy should be the weapon of openness."*
>
> *- Niels Bohr*
> *1922 Nobel Prize Winner in Physics*

I have always been a pretty transparent and open leader. Not that I am sharing intimate details of my personal life or political or religious opinions, rather the kind of leader that talks openly about the business, admits mistakes, raises awareness of external concerns and tries to have the humility to be open to criticism from my team. As a result, I like to think my teams trust me and give me the straight goods, no matter how screwed up the situation might be.

I find if you can be open and transparent, you quickly build trust and if you build trust, your team will do whatever it takes to succeed. But I have learned over the years that openness and transparency are not appreciated in command and control environments. Mistakes are covered up and buried away in inaccessible locations. Reality is often overridden by deceit and lies which cannot be questioned or justified. I can barely remember a meeting in my 30+ years of working that anyone was ever asked to show the supporting documentation to support a claim.

In command and control, information is either completely disorganized or simply locked down for fear of someone finding some information that they are not privy to. I heard a statistic that said the average knowledge base worker spends 1/3 of their time looking for information. That's more than a day and a half per week wasted because we don't take the time to organize information or we put unnecessary controls in place limiting access to crucial information!

People need access to information to make good decisions and I help them organize their information in a way that is secure yet transparent, easily allowing access to each stakeholder and team member while keeping others out. In an emergency, the faster the information can be accessed, the less impact the emergency will have on the organization.

Openness is a key driver to team accountability and without proper consideration and willingness to be open, teams will continue to hide mistakes, lie about their progress and deceive stakeholders. High-performance teams that want to create holistic solutions understand the importance of letting others review their work, and incorporate it into their own responsibilities. If you feel that people are not accountable, ask yourself if they are being open? Openness is no longer a grudging obligation, it's an opportunity to empower people, enhance collaboration and continuously do the right thing.

10. Changing to an Accountable Culture

> *"There is no chance, no destiny, no fate that can circumvent or hinder or control the firm resolve of a determined soul."*
>
> - Ella Wilcox
>
> Author and poet

When you commit to creating a culture of accountability in your organization, you will begin to see an incremental transformation. It starts slowly. Visible signs of early success may be simple things like people showing up earlier and leaving later, enjoying themselves at work, laughter in meetings, salutations in the hallways or lively conversation in the elevator.

If you can create an accountable culture, people will love being part of it, then as you get better at it, they will perform at a higher level. There will be less conflict and babysitting. There will be improved consideration for other's challenges and cross-functional support. There will be lower levels of workplace injuries and turnover and higher levels of quality, creativity, and innovation.

Accountability is not about focusing on punishing people who have lied, cheated or were ignorant of needs and expectations. It's not about fixing the mistakes of the past. It's about accepting those mistakes as being a symptom of the top-down management model and a willingness to move on; to do what's right from this point forward.

An accountable culture can boost results and reduce organizational losses at every level and in every corner and crevice of your business. Whatever you do, you can do better, with a workforce who has been freed from command and control management practices; a workforce who doesn't cower when bullies walk into the room and a workforce who no longer believes that the path to success is being that hero who runs over people to get the task done.

Once the principles begin to take hold, your team will be able to more clearly see where they can improve results and reduce losses. The world of chaos will fade away, allowing you to see the root causes of your organizational challenges and deal with them, rather than the symptoms. And dealing with root causes will then create higher levels of commitment. People will see you are willing to get rid of the challenges that hold them back or hold them down. A continuous upward spiral of success will follow the initial improvement in attitude and your organization will simply get better and better.

If you still don't think making people more accountable at work is worth your time, be warned, the workplace is changing. People want to be managed differently today. They want autonomy to innovate and be respected at an individual level. They don't want to abdicate control of their work to their boss or the departmental bully and they don't want the perks often associated with success, such as the corner office of premium parking spots. They simply want to be left alone and allowed to do the best they can and contribute to the success of the team.

In a Gallup global benchmark survey[10] of over 200,000 worldwide workers, they found only 13% were engaged in their work, meaning they are involved in, enthusiastic about and committed to their work and workplace. That lack of enthusiasm for what we do is a chronic symptom of command and control. People do what they do because they have been told to, not because they understand why they are doing it or the importance of the task and how it contributes to the overall vision and success of the organization.

Today's workforce wants their opinions to be considered. Decision-making and idea generation should no longer be the privilege of the higher-ups. Today's workforce wants their initiatives to be noticed and supported, not set aside in a drawer of ideas. They want their management to recognize the value they bring and help to nurture and support them through skill development and training, by opening doors and removing obstacles and by acting as a cheerleader and motivator, not an oppressor.

The old command and control management style of hoarding power and decision-making among the organizational elite is increasingly at odds with society; a society that is embracing the power of the consumer.

I recently signed up with Uber and requested a ride on their smartphone app. The instant I hit the button to order my ride, the app told me how far away my driver was, who they were and what kind of vehicle they were driving. The drivers tended to be very personable and committed to the customer experience.

When the trip was finished, payment was automatic, and a pop up asked for feedback on the driver and the vehicle (apparently the drivers can also rate the passengers to hold them accountable as well). On one ride, the car was quite loud and there was little legroom in the back. I reported this and within hours had a customer service representative contacting me to ask me more about my concerns. This level of service, accountability, and results does not exist in the command and control culture of the traditional taxi company.

On another trip, my phone had died so when I arrived at the airport, I queued up at the taxi stand and caught a ride with a regular cab. The minivan, although not particularly clean was acceptable by cab standards. As we left the airport and took the on-ramp to the local expressway, I noticed a significant shake in the vehicle. I commented to the driver that he needed to get that looked at.

A few minutes later, the rear tire exploded. My heart jumped, and I grabbed on to whatever I could to brace myself for imminent danger as the driver maneuvered across four lanes of 75 mile an hour traffic before safely coming to a stop on the shoulder. My driver called for another taxi to pick me up and when they arrived 20 minutes later (the airport was only 10 minutes away) they told me they would transfer the meter charge from the first taxi to the second.

I told them that I was not going to pay for the first ride. The taxi was not maintained properly, and they had put my life in danger because of that lack of maintenance. The driver checked with dispatch and was told that if I was not willing to pay, they were going to leave me on the side of the highway! Talk about no accountability!

Organizations that do not embrace a more collaborative and accountable business model are not adapting to the changes that are happening in society. They are becoming increasingly decoupled from a world of employees that wants to be treated, not as someone special, but as someone important; someone who contributes to the organization's bottom line and they want to be held accountable, in the case of Uber, for a clean, well-maintained vehicle and an awesome customer experience.

The emerging organizational model is one that not only improves the customer experience but the employee experience as well. The personality, engagement, and enthusiasm of every Uber driver I have had was markedly better than that of their command and control counterparts.

Today's workforce does not want to be "managed". They do not want to work under an authoritative slave driver who has little capacity for personal initiative, have all the answers and tell everyone what to do and how to do it. They are not easily swayed by traditional punishment and reward systems and do not work well when looking at their coworkers as rivals. They look at coworkers as collaborative team members, not enemies.

I am by no means advocating for the elimination of managers, although some organizations have taken that path. Google spent many years pondering the question of whether managers were required at all. Their conclusion was that they were indeed important in driving increased employee satisfaction, improving morale and achieving results, but the role of the manager needed to change from overlord to mentor and facilitator. From taskmaster to visionary leader, anticipating the challenges that lay ahead and removing them proactively, so the team could focus on getting stuff done.

Many managers today can't change, or perhaps more accurately don't want to change. They grew up and thrived in the command and control culture. They withheld their opinions and ideas for years waiting for their turn to be the boss; the one who can now make all the decisions. They don't want to turn around and give up that hard-earned right to boss people around…they have earned it.

Can we challenge the habits of the past? Can we expect today's leaders to change? Or should we jump ship to find more progressive leaders in other industries?

I met with a local executive recently who felt that most organizational leaders don't have the self-awareness to admit to a shortcoming or gap, let alone be open to a different approach to management. Many claim to be "fiercely independent" and think that accountability will take away their ability to do whatever it takes to succeed. And they might be right, to some degree.

But accountability is something we all do. Anyone who has excelled at their role in any organization or industry are typically the ones who can drive higher levels of accountability. They are able to get all their team, including those die-hard, old-school managers, to embrace a collaborative culture that provides clarity on responsibilities and expectations and holds people to their commitments.

By embracing a more accountable approach, these managers often find themselves freed from dealing with petty problems and can now go after bigger issues and become a service provider to their customers, following up to concerns or complaints, such as the Uber manager who reached out to me. Or removing potential challenges and obstacles from the path of their team.

The most difficult challenge may be the need to embrace your employees or your volunteers as highly valuable, intelligent people who need to be trusted and respected. This seemingly utopian approach is easily dismissed by those who have spent their lives being treated poorly; being questioned for their motives; their intelligence; and their commitment.

Embracing a philosophy that believes that people are good, want to do the right thing and want their organizations to succeed is a big stretch for managers. A workplace study in France found that only 4% of executives believed their workforces had the intelligence and skills needed to drive success.

Yet, trust and respect of the workforce have been found to be a cornerstone in many of the organizations that are challenging the status quo. Trusting and respecting individual responsibilities puts the pressure on the team and the individual to perform and takes away the excuses and apathy that has plagued our workforce. When bosses are bossy, you simply do what you are told…that's it.

By removing the murkiness of command and control and replacing it with the transparency of accountability, the worker's ability to do their job increases, as does the manager's ability to monitor the success of the work, resulting in improved customer and employee satisfaction and organizational growth, while reducing organizational overhead (less overlap of responsibilities), work interruptions, injuries and staff turnover. Simply put, happy workers ensure satisfied customers ensure healthy organizations.

But with such an amazing value proposition, why aren't organizations rushing to embrace a more accountable approach to how they do their work? In a word, **EGO**. The term ego is often used but rarely understood. Ego is the mediator between societal norms and expectations and our ideal selves. As a result, most people act in a way that is not necessarily in alignment with their true desire but with societal assumptions and stereotypes.

In today's work world, being competitive is more valued than being collaborative, so people tend to be that way simply because it is expected, not necessarily that they agree with it or are even good at it. Societal stereotypes, such as being demanding, is considered a strength while being empathetic, the act of truly understanding an issue and its impacts, is considered a weakness.

As a result, most people's outward self is highly influenced by the culture that already exists. If the dominant culture is based on bullies and heroes, then an individual takes a significant risk by acting otherwise.

To change existing cultural norms, it is critical that we;

1) Empathize with those in our organization who have let you down in the past and agree to move forward with a new focus on improving the quality of our relationships and our culture of accountability. By understanding how their behavior has been shaped by social expectation and norms of the past opens the door to change those expectations and norms.

2) Look at our own actions and ask, "What do we do to reinforce those organizational norms?" Every successful change initiative begins with examining our own behavior to be more conscious of the things we do to reinforce the current culture. Through this enhanced consciousness, we begin to separate our true self from the social expectations that we try to live up to.

3) Create safe environments based on trust and mutual respect that will encourage people, even in key leadership roles, to be open and share stories about how the culture affected them, perhaps before they got into their position of authority and leadership.

4) Embrace the process of creating powerful, cohesive teams. Life is so much better when you work with people you trust and believe in. People who are there for you and willingly accept help when you are there for them.

I believe **Accountable** will guide you through the process, but you must be willing and able to challenge even the content of this book in your own organization. There is no one process to move from the chaos of a competitive command and control culture to the clarity of an accountable team culture.

This book can provide guidance and support for your organization's transition to high-performance, but it is not a silver bullet. It will help you change your mindset and your attitude, but it will take time, commitment to the process, and courage to change your organizational culture.

You must have a powerful guiding vision that your team will buy into. A vision strong enough to ensure that you and your team will be willing to move from;

- Silos to integrated systems
- Autocratic rule to distributed leadership
- Arm's length relationships to mutual collaboration
- Enforcement to empowerment

Change is never easy. I remember when I was a young marketing engineer working for a very progressive company in the late 1980's. I worked in the sales and marketing group which was likely the most progressive of all the divisions. We embraced a culture that was not locked in the past including radical new technologies, like the desktop computer!

When I was promoted to the machining division, the culture was still dominated by the old guard and when I first powered up my desktop computer that I had brought with me from sales, one of the old boys sneered from my doorway, "I see you brought your typewriter with you. When are you going to start wearing a f*#%ing skirt to work?"

I could have changed myself to meet the social and gender expectations by turning my computer off and going back to doing handwritten notes that were then transferred to one of the secretaries to type up, but I refused. I knew that going back to that old-school approach would limit my ability meet my customer and stakeholder needs so I refused. I risked social and organizational rejection from my peers and leaders because I knew that a computer made me better.

In doing so, I was one of many people shifting social expectations and making a positive difference. Organizational norms, whether they are based on gender, age, or position are deeply entrenched in our society and trying to shift them is no easy task. By embracing a more accountable approach that respects each team member and the importance of their role in achieving organizational success, people can step up and contribute to the organization's success in a bigger way.

It's time we stop accepting the mediocrity and chaos of the command and control culture and recognize the value and importance of embracing a more accountable team culture that empowers and leverages the strength and ability of each team member. It's time to drop the increasingly ineffective and inefficient model and replace it with a more inspirational one that allows organizations to get the most out of their people.

I encourage each of you to be a leader, willing to take the risks associated with moving away from your organizational norms and beginning the process of building a culture of accountability. And I encourage you to share this book with your leaders, run a book review and get accountability on the radar of every executive, manager, and employee across the organization.

Accountability is the glue that makes commitment stick and results happen.

Notes

1. "The HOW Report: A Global, Empirical Analysis of How Governance, Culture, and Leadership Impact Performance" LRN Group, 2016.

2. "ERBI 2008 Recent Retirees Survey: Report of Findings" Employee Benefit Research Group, Issue Brief No. 319, July 2008.

3. "Workplace Review: Calgary Police Service", Deborah E Prowse, QC, November 2013.

4. "U.S. Household net worth graphic", Wikipedia, March 11, 2010.

5. "Healthy People, Healthy Places", Statistics Canada, September 28, 2016.

6. "Mastering Civility, a Manifesto for the Workplace", Christine Porath, Grand Central Publishing, December 2016.

7. "Dismal Employee Engagement Is a Sign of Global Mismanagement", Gallup Blog, December 20, 2017.

8. "Complicatedness Survey: What's Bogging Down Your Business?" Boston Consulting Group.

9. "Fixit; Getting Accountability Right" Connors, Smith, Hickman, Skouse, & Nicolls, Portfolio / Penguin, 2016.

10. "Managerial Leadership and Ischaemic Heart Disease Among Employees: The Swedish WOLF Study" Nyberg, Alfredsson, Theorell, Westerlund, Vahtera, Kivimäki, Department of Public Health Sciences, Karolinska Institute, SE-171 77 Stockholm, Sweden, January 2009. anna.nyberg@ki.se

11. “Work-unit measures of organisational justice and risk of depression: a 2-year cohort study” Grynderup, Mors, Hansen, Andersen, Bonde, Kærgaard, Kærlev, Mikkelsen, Rugulies, Thomsen, Kolstad, Department of Occupational Medicine, Danish Ramazzini Centre, Aarhus University Hospital, Aarhus, Denmark, June 2013. matigryn@rm.dk.

12. “Why I Love Micromanaging and You Should Too” Jack Welch, LinkedIn, January 19, 2016.

13. “Trust Works! Four Keys to Building Lasting Relationships”, Blanchard, Olmstead, Lawrence, Harper Collins, 2013.

About the Author

Peter (Pete) Myers has been labeled a lot of things, including rebel, critic, his own worst enemy and Mr. Accountability. Never to succumb to the pressures of the boy's club or willing to accept the status quo, Pete has consistently pushed to create win-win solutions that go beyond the needs of his boss or boss' boss, even when he has been told not to!

A mechanical engineer with a master's degree in education, and a life's experience managing projects across numerous industries, Peter's unique focus has always been on how to make the workplace a more enjoyable and productive place through the empowerment of people, integration of systems and alignment of resources.

As CEO of Mesh Organizational Services, Pete provides training and consulting services to help teams be more accountable to their customers, to their leadership and most importantly, to each other.

Pete holds a BASc degree in Mechanical Engineering from the University of Windsor, and a Master's degree (MA) in education from Royal Roads University, where he focused on revolutionizing our education systems through recognition of informal learning, implementation of peer-peer learning systems and the development of skill and knowledge sharing networks.

Pete lives in Calgary and has two boys hitting puberty! He is a member of the Choirboys Old-timers Hockey Club and is an avid mountain biker and Past-President of the Fernie Mountain Bike Club.

He is also passionate about giving back through volunteerism and is the incoming President for the APEGA Foundation, a not-for-profit that inspires and empowers engineers and geoscientists in Alberta to make a difference.

He can be reached at pete@mesh.team.

Made in the USA
Monee, IL
23 November 2019

17339998R00069